Building My Yellow Brick Road:

Life Lessons from Pursuing a Dream

By Melissa Thomas

To Diane,
#dreamsmatter
Pursue Them!
♡ Melissa

For Braden and Nathan –

Let no one tell you that your dreams are unattainable. Do not believe them when they say your dreams are dumb, stupid, or crazy. My prayer is for you to pursue your God-given dreams and learn your own life lessons.

For all my CCHS kids –

It was my privilege to be your teacher and your mentor. It is my honor to be your friend.

I have loved watching you all grow up and pursue your own dreams. This book is especially written to the memory of our Katie, who taught us to persevere despite the struggles, to overcome the obstacles and most importantly, to always have a positive attitude and a smile!

"Nothing is as real as a dream. The world can change around you, but your dream will not. Responsibilities need not erase it. Duties need not obscure it. Because the dream is within you, no one can take it away."
Tom Clancy

<u>What Others Are Saying...</u>

"The author, Melissa Thomas, loves Elton John. She tells a charming yet motivating story highlighting her journey to meet Elton John but it's clearly a vehicle for her ordinary life which she finally realizes is an extraordinary life. That's one of her Life Lessons that she has peppered throughout the book and which she has garnered on her journey to being debt free. Maybe your passion isn't about Elton John but that's not the point Melissa is making—it's about what YOU are passionate about and how you pursue that passion. Underneath her desire to meet Elton John she quietly shows us how she guided her family to being debt free, that she is her own person, and has a realistic, happy, grounded marriage, and a beautiful family along with many friends. It's work, it's taking action. it's sticking to a plan. Her book clearly explains how a person can follow their dreams all the while doing the right thing at the right time the right way. It's an inspirational book because she highlights the life lessons she's learned through following Elton.

Melissa's account of his reminded me of so many of the songs I grew up with in the late 60s when Elton wore his "Liberace"—his outrageous—costumes. It was a walk down Memory Lane to remember the evolution of Elton and see the evolution of Melissa. The essence of Melissa's book is captured in the lyrics of one of her favorite songs by Elton, The Bridge, "Do you cross the bridge or do you fade away?" Do you follow your dreams whatever they are or do you let them fade away? How many of us can say that we turn our dreams into reality? Do you do the work to achieve your goals? Read Building My Yellow Brick Road and get inspired."

Pattie Rydlun, Keynote Speaker and Business Coach

"I have been a student of personal and professional development for over 25 years and have read hundreds of books. I thoroughly enjoyed reading "Building My Yellow Brick Road". Melissa captivates you with her story telling abilities and reveals her vulnerability and authentic self. I was inspired by her dedication to stay true to herself and not let anyone nor anything get in the way of pursuing her dream. Being a part of the progression to this dream, she is able to give insights and thought provoking ideas that we can all apply to our own hopes and dreams. She makes any and all dreams that we have become valid and important. The book is an encouragement to many, and I highly recommend that you learn from the valuable life lessons shared."

Loretta Koeth, National Marketing Director,
The Juice Plus Company

"Dreams. How many of us have been laughed at, mocked, even shunned for our dreams? I love how Melissa gives us permission, even dares us, to believe that our dreams do matter, regardless of what others say. "Building my Yellow Brick Road" has so many valuable nuggets and the life lessons at the end of each chapter really gave me the nudge to reflect on my own journey of pursuing my dreams. This journey is all about learning from life experiences: both the victories and defeats. Melissa's transparency allows us to celebrate the victories of overcoming the defeats! If you have a dream and a heart's desire, this book is a must read!"

Melissa Martin, Business Coach and
Network Marketing Professional

Contents

Introduction 9

1 The New Reality 13

2 The Beginning 19

3 Trash Can Dreams 23

4 Common Sense 29

5 Adulting 33

6 Perspective 37

7 Leaving the Comfort Zone 41

8 The Big Picture 45

9 The One 49

10 Someday, Out of the Blue 57

11 Look Out, New World 59

12 The Turning Point 63

13 Problem Solving, Part 1 69

14 Persistence and Perseverance 71

15 The Vision Becomes Reality 77

16 Cramming 83

17 Crowd Control 89

18 Problem Solving, Part 2 91

19 The Solution 95

20 Opportunity Knocks 99

21 Purpose 107

22 People Are People 109

23 One More Try 117

24 Moving Forward 127

25 Living the Life 131

26 The Unforgettable Moment 137

27 We're Debt-Free! 141

28 Personality Flaw 145

29 Friends 149

30 That's Not Good Enough 165

31 My Not-So-Ordinary Life 173

Epilogue 177

Concert List 181

Acknowledgements 183

Introduction

For years, my friends and family have encouraged me to put my stories in a book—particularly my most epic concert adventures. I started writing in 2014, jotting the stories down on paper as I remembered them. Initially, I wrote them down for my sons (they have lived through many of these stories, but I'm not sure how much they remember). As they got older, I wanted them to have something tangible to read when I was no longer around to tell the stories. However, over the past few years, the encouragement to write has grown stronger. I had no idea how to write a book, even though I'd spent many years reading them. I thought I couldn't write a book because I am not an author. My friend Matt Ham, who is a published author, told me, "You are not an author until you write something." This made perfect sense to me. I suppose I just needed to hear it said aloud. And, yes, I needed that encouragement.

There is such a conflict in writing a book: how much or how little do I put in there? What do people want to read? Will they buy my book if I add this or don't add that? Should I worry about that? After all, it is my story—everything should be included, right? But it's such a dichotomy of opposites—the pursuit of my dream and my faith that the very God I believe in was instrumental in everything that happened along this journey. How do I write a book that intertwines my conviction in the teachings of the Roman Catholic faith and my pursuit of meeting Elton John? Will people be offended? Will they boycott my book? Should I add in those parts of how God put certain people and circumstances into my life to allow me to get as far as I have in my pursuit?

I struggled with this when I first thought about writing the book, and I thought about it while I wrote it. Even after I sent it to my editor, the nudging continued—did I include too much or too little? What happens if I ignore the nudging and I don't include it? What should I do?

It's a question I ignored for too long and ultimately, I received my answer while listening to the radio. My answer was in the song "My Story" by Big Daddy Weave. The first time I heard that song, my mind went through the lyrics and these thoughts came to mind:

Through the years, I have maintained hope that my dream is worth pursuing.

My love for the pursuit of the dream taught me to never give up.

This dream is not just my dream; it is a dream for everyone who dares to do so. I inspire and encourage others to pursue their dreams.

I have had protection and safety in all my travels. Unexpected things that just happen to get me one step closer. I know Jesus was watching over me.

I firmly believe that this is a God-given dream, one I am meant to pursue as God has put the people in my life I need along the way. Debt stood in the way, so we met it head-on and won victory over it.

This isn't just a story of faith. It isn't just a story about Elton John, and it isn't just a story of my life. It is all those things and more woven together in the story of a journey. It's a story written from my memory, with the help of friends, and it's a story of a journey to find the bricks to build my own Yellow Brick Road.

1
The New Reality

August 2016

Drive to one concert, fly to the other three, but fly, then drive. I need a rental car.

Fly into one airport, fly home from another.

Eight nights in hotels.

Four concerts in six states over nine days.

Concert tickets for four different concerts in four different cities.

Four different outfits, but the same pair of shoes. Oh, yes, my beloved black Doc Marten shoes. The same shoes I've worn to every concert since about 2001.

Pack one bag for the driving trip.

Pack another bag for the flying trip.

Don't forget the tickets. Go put the tickets in the suitcase right now.

Bring four different items for autographs—what should I bring?

Make a poster—one poster for four different shows. The green poster board. I used that last time and he saw it. Consistency is key.

Don't forget the cardboard travel tube for the flight. And the black marker for the poster.

And the black markers for autographs. I always buy those brand new.

Plan for me to be out of town for six days—after all, I am also the household manager (AKA wife and mom) and need to be sure the household logistics are secured.

I need a business plan for six days of vacation—after all, I own a business too, and am the sole employee. Create an auto-reply that I am out of town pursuing my dream, but I'll still be available via email and text. I have clients who need me even when I'm away.

• • • •

The effort needed to organize an Elton John concert trip adventure would deter most people from even making the attempt. You'd think I'd have this routine down by now, given I've attended thirty-two concerts so far. But I don't. Each trip is different. That's part of what makes it so exciting. To me, no matter the logistics, every moment I spend planning and organizing is worth it. After all, this is a big dream I am pursuing, and making dreams come true isn't an easy task.

Ah, the crazy logistics of pursuing a dream. This, however, is my new reality. The reality of attending multiple concerts at time, most in different states and often requiring a flight reservation, and always sitting on the first three rows.

Six years ago, you couldn't have convinced me that any of this was even possible. Well, maybe the first of the four upcoming shows, but certainly not the last three. Those are three states away and I need to fly there (well, I don't *need* to, but the older I get, the harder it is to make those long road trips). Plus, I'd have to be away from home longer. I love to travel, but I also have a family and a business that need me at home.

Six years ago, we were living paycheck-to-paycheck, had no money in savings, and no plan for our financial future. We had over $43,500 of consumer debt. I had spent too many years allowing money to be the thing that stood in the way of me and my dream.

Six years ago, I'd had enough. I was done. But here I am now, more than twenty years after attending my first Elton John concert, adding yet another set of concerts to my list. It's the first time I've attended four concerts in one short span of time, but not my first time attending multiple concerts. It's not the first time I've flown to concerts, either, but it is the first time I fly into one state and attend three concerts while I'm there.

I've come a long way since my first concert that was just a short, twenty-minute drive from my home. So much has changed, and yet some things have remained the same. Some things I thought to be impossible have since become possible. There have been so many life lessons and unintended consequences.

It's one thing to have a dream. It's another to act on it, to pursue it. It takes determination, grit, and a certain attitude of a chip on your shoulder, or *chutzpah*. Pursuing a dream means overcoming obstacles, finding my people, and somewhere along the way, believing enough in myself that I can do it.

I was only nineteen years old when I attended my first Elton John concert. I had no idea at the time how much that one decision would impact my life. Who I am now is not who I was at nineteen. And yet, my dream—to one day meet Elton John in person—has not changed. There have been times when that dream got moved aside, but it's been more in front of me the older I have become. Because the older I get, the older Elton gets, and he's more than twenty-five years my senior. Time is of the essence with my dream. There is an expiration date—either when I meet Elton and achieve the dream, or when it's his time to go from this earth to Heaven.

This tour is supposed to be his "early retirement" tour. Supposedly, he's not going to tour as extensively as he has in the past. I guess it will mean fewer trips "across the pond" to the United States. What does that mean for me? I will just have to renew my passport and start saving for that trip to Europe I've always wanted to take.

There's another thing I wouldn't have given much thought to six years ago. It's hard to make plans like that while trying to keep ahead of bills, save money, and stop "robbing Peter to pay Paul." It's hard to imagine a life beyond my life six years ago, when I was a stay-at-home mom to two boys, thirteen months apart. Six years ago, they were five and four. The only thing they have ever known about money is the life we have *now*. That's so crazy to write that and re-read it. I say it so often, but to write it down seems weird. More on that in a later chapter.

Right now, my life is mired in trip planning, running my company, and being the wife and mom and friend and family member. (Eh, *mired* isn't the right word. That sounds so negative. I am abundantly blessed with these things.) Right now, I'm sitting in the quietness of our home office. The boys are in bed, my husband isn't home from work yet, and the dogs have settled in for the night. I get to sit in my air-conditioned house in the middle of August and share my story. My story that has already inspired so many who have been there or have followed along.

My story is one I hope will inspire you to learn from the lessons I have learned so you, too, can pursue your dream—whatever that may be.

2
<u>The Beginning</u>

I grew up listening to all the folk groups of the '60s and '70s. I don't remember the first song I ever heard, but I do remember singing along to "Puff the Magic Dragon" by Peter, Paul, and Mary as a young child. For as far back as I can recall, I have always loved music. And dogs—I have always loved dogs. But this isn't a story about dogs. It's a story about how my curiosity and the love of music came together to form a dream.

I was born in 1973, the oldest of three children. My mom was a teacher; my dad was a computer engineer. Of course, I didn't know at the time, but there was another pretty big event in 1973—one that I would later define as *fate*, or *karma*, or whatever you want to call it.

I don't recall a time when I didn't love music. It was only in listening to it, though, because I never learned how to play an instrument. But I knew how to work a boom box, and it was this skill that came in handy the day I was perusing through a box of my dad's cassette tapes. I found one that piqued my curiosity. The cover art was so fascinating to me—it was a picture of a man stepping onto a Yellow Brick Road.

Of course, I knew all about the Yellow Brick Road from the movie *The Wizard of Oz*, but I hadn't heard of this singer before, and this was the very first time I intentionally listened to his music. It was the song titles that intrigued me, so I popped the cassette into the boom box and hit play. Time and age have clouded the memory of the first song I ever heard, but I will never forget the feeling that overcame me—that voice, the music of the one and only Sir Elton John.

I know I listened to the whole cassette from beginning to end, and then again as I learned the words to all the songs. I was a brand-new teenager living in a middle-class household, and Elton John was my new favorite musician. It was the late '80s,, and to say that Elton John wasn't exactly the most popular artist among all the other girls my age is a total understatement. But, then again, I wasn't the most popular with all the other teenage girls, either.

I was different. I had copper-red hair, wore glasses, and I wasn't a girly-girl. I was a tomboy. I loved sports and disliked school. I wasn't into boys and dating and all that other stuff that teenage girls are into. I just wanted to go to school and get through class so I could go to volleyball, basketball, or softball practice, depending on the season. I wasn't particularly good at sports, but I loved playing. I loved the competition.

My life pretty much centered around my sports and my dog. Her name was Bijou. It was a vocabulary word I'd learned in French class, and I thought it was such a cool name for a dog. When I was in high school, I wanted to be a veterinarian, so I spent a *lot* of time in the biology teacher's classroom because she had all the animals.

Yes, I was just different from everyone else. Maybe that's what first got me hooked on the music, because it was different, too.

Once I fell in love with the music, I had to know more about the man behind it. I learned there were more albums than *Goodbye Yellow Brick Road*, and I did whatever I could to get them. The more I listened, the more in love I fell with the music. I learned to love the man behind the music, too—and not just him, but his talent and his story. His life story that is so inspiring. The story that would challenge me in my own religious beliefs and values, and force me to stand up for *my* dreams and *my* passions.

At some point, I learned that Elton performed his music live in concert, and I set about planning to go. Little did I know at the time how much that one decision to go see him perform would impact my life in such a big way.

I was born the same year *Goodbye Yellow Brick Road* was released, 1973. Call it fate, or karma, or whatever, but many people live their whole life without a dream or knowing their purpose. I've lived more years with a dream than without one. My dream has indirectly led me to my purpose. There have been some crazy adventures along the way, and I've been told they have inspired others to pursue their dreams, too. I am the Rocket Man Fan, and this is my story.

Life Lesson:
Be curious and act on that curiosity. You never know what curiosity will inspire.

3
Trash Can Dreams

I spent most of my childhood living in Raleigh, North Carolina. This was fortunate for me, because it's a decent-sized city with an amphitheater for a concert venue. That amphitheater would become a stop on Elton John's *The One* tour.

By this time, I had already spent my high school years as a huge fan of Elton John. I was once assigned a project in music class to write a report on a musician. I told my teacher I wanted to write about Elton John. She didn't want me to at first, but I pleaded my case. I won on the condition that I do the report on something other than just his history.

The resistance? I was a student at a Catholic high school. My favorite musician was Elton John. If you know anything about the Catholic faith, being a fan of Elton and attending Catholic school didn't exactly go together, especially in the early '90s.

So my report centered around his music and his musical partnership with Bernie Taupin. I remember making a tape of various pieces of his piano playing from the songs for my classmates to listen to as I finished my report. Doing a report on Elton John and his various styles of piano playing sure didn't help my popularity at all, but I loved doing the task at hand, and I am grateful for my teacher who allowed me that privilege.

After I graduated from Catholic high school, I followed my faith and attended a Catholic college. Of course, I moved into the dorm with my boom box and my Elton John cassettes and CDs. I declared a major in biology with plans to pursue a degree in veterinary medicine after my undergraduate work was complete. I had known since I was old enough to know what a veterinarian was that this profession was what I wanted to do. I went to college very intent on my life's path, my dream—to pursue a passion of caring for animals, especially dogs.

After completing my first year of college, I returned home for the summer—home to my city with that decent-sized amphitheater. That amphitheater would become stop one on Elton John's *The One* tour. If Elton was coming to *my* city, you can be sure I wanted to be there, too!

My parents told me I could go if I could find someone older than me to go with me. At the time, I was working for a dog groomer, so I asked my boss, Kim, if she would like to go. She agreed. Assuming we bought the tickets from Ticketmaster, we ended up in the last row under the overhang, about forty rows from the stage. (You should understand that at this point, I didn't even care *where* I was sitting, I was just so happy to be in the same space as Elton John.)

Before the show, I'd bought a wall poster of the album cover for *The One* from the merchandise table. I went on to spend most of the time holding it under the overhang as best I could, because it rained that night. There was a plastic sleeve over the poster, but it was the first thing I'd ever bought at an Elton concert and therefore, a most prized possession.

A few weeks after the show, I took that poster to a professional frame shop and very carefully picked out a gold frame. As if the teasing in high school and college about being such a huge Elton John fan and subsequent quizzical looks about actually going to see Elton in concert weren't enough, I spent quite a bit of my hard-earned money working at the dog groomer's to have the poster professionally framed. Certainly, no big box poster frame was going to be good enough for this poster. It had to be special, so I chose a gold-colored, metal frame and a large piece of glass to protect this prized souvenir. That professionally-framed poster eventually went back to college with me, then, to my first, second, and third apartments, and finally to our current home, where it hangs on the hallway wall today.

I attended my first Elton concert in 1992. I no longer remember all the details, but I will never forget the feeling that came over me when the lights went off and the music started. The first few notes from the electronic keyboard began to play "Funeral for a Friend." Of course, I knew it well from the *Goodbye Yellow Brick Road* album.

Imagine this: it's a September evening in North Carolina, which means it's a little humid and the sun has just set. The weather is rainy and overcast, enhancing the atmosphere. The venue holds just over twenty thousand people, and the show is close to sold out. There's not an empty seat as far as I can see.

Stage lights cast a glow around the amphitheater, but the entire venue goes dark right before Elton John walks out onto the stage. Almost simultaneously, the crowd begins to cheer. Not a loud cheer at first, but more of a, "Hooray, the concert is getting ready to start!" cheer. Some people are still chatting or finding their seats; not everyone is focused on the stage until the first few notes of "Love Lies Bleeding/Funeral for a Friend" come on and you see the smoke start to roll across the stage. Then, the noise of the cheering crowd becomes louder; people are clapping and cheering and watching the stage.

When Elton John ascends to the top of the stairs on the side of the stage, the wave of eruption begins as people realize what is happening. The applause and the clapping is so loud it's like thunder multiplied a thousand times. Elton walks across and to the front of the stage, waving to the crowd, then turns and walks to the piano. With a few strokes of the keys on that Yamaha concert grand piano, the concert begins.

I was so overcome with emotion that this moment was finally happening that when Elton John walked out onto the stage and the crowd erupted in applause, I cried. I mean, I *cried*. You know, the tears of happiness because you're just so darn happy that the moment you have been waiting for finally happened? Yes, that kind of cried. I'm sure I probably cried throughout the entire show. (You should know that I am not a crier. I have this innate ability to always keep my emotions in check, especially when it comes to crying.)

I know for sure that I screamed and yelled and sang—oh, yes, I sang! (Because no one could hear me. I am not blessed with a singing voice, and yet, I discovered that at a concert, I can sing as loud as I want because Elton and the band and the crowd are louder and no one can hear me.) I know all the words to all the songs, so why wouldn't I sing?

Although my seat was in the last row under the overhang, which was closer than all the people sitting in the rows of chairs and lawn area behind me, I couldn't help but notice all the people who were sitting right in front of the stage, in the front row! I was astounded that they were *that* close to the stage, *that* close to Elton John. Suddenly, although I was so happy just to be at that concert, I was no longer happy with my seat underneath the awning. I wanted a front-row seat!

I was nineteen years old and didn't know much about visualization or dream boards or the idea of calling a certain thing into your life, but I found a seat, center stage, row one, and I imagined myself sitting there, in that seat, just a few steps from the edge of the stage. I imagined what it would be like to be that close to Elton and the band.

One of my favorite things about seeing Elton live in concert is that the songs are different. No, the lyrics and the tune are the same, but there is a lot more musical liberty taken with a live performance than that of one recorded for an album. This concert was the first time I heard the song "Rocket Man" performed live. One line, "I think it's gonna be a long, long time," sounded so different and energetic performed live. It's also the first time I heard the "Rocket Man" echo—it's something I've only heard in live performances. Elton sings, "I'm a rocket man," and the words *rocket man* echo and echo and echo. It was the most awesome singing sound effect I have ever heard. You can hear it for yourself by googling "Elton John Rocket Man 60th Concert" and having a listen!

I knew then that I would be a fan of Elton John for a "long, long time." It was at this show that I also determined two things:

1. I wanted to be one of "those people" in a front-row seat.
2. I wanted to meet Elton John in person.

I was nineteen years old, I had a dream, and it wasn't one I was going to throw in the trash.

Life Lesson:
Experiences create dreams. Live a life of experiences.

4
Common Sense

Anyone who has ever had a dream, a goal, a purpose, or a mission will tell you that sometimes things are crazy. People tell you you're crazy, that your dream is crazy. That you have flat-out lost your common sense. Well, at least that happened to me.

It made no sense that I could accomplish my dream to meet Elton John in person. Who did I think I was, having that kind of a dream? I was a nineteen-year-old girl getting ready to start her sophomore year in college with a track that would take me from an undergraduate degree to a graduate degree, and on to spending the rest of my life as a veterinarian. I was the oldest of three from a middle-class family with absolutely no connections to the music industry. I was a born and raised Roman Catholic, from a long line of Catholics—both Irish and Italian—and I had decided that my huge life dream was to meet Elton John in person. Like, be standing across from him and shake his hand. Maybe even have a picture taken!

In the beginning, I told everyone my dream; I was *so* excited! But, after enough people told me I was crazy—and yes, even some who said it was a dumb, stupid dream—I sort of packed it away for a while. I know now that, at that point in my life, I had just not found the right people who would believe in my dream as much as I did. That's not to say I didn't have supporters; it is to say I just didn't have the right kind of supporters—the people who would really believe in me and not just tell me what I wanted to hear, even if they didn't believe it. I allowed myself to put my dream in a little box of sorts. I would always have it. It was always there—never forgotten about, but just not verbalized as much.

Turns out, not everyone around me was as excited about my dream. It's kind of hard to maintain enthusiasm when no one around you is either pursuing the same thing or supporting it. I was just at the very early stages of figuring out how to be an adult at this point, trying to find my way and map out my future.

In 1993, I attended my second Elton John concert. I was in college, and traveled to Chapel Hill, North Carolina, for the show. My mom and dad went with me, and for the first time I had balcony seats. Imagine my great joy when we discovered we were in the front row of the balcony seats, overlooking Elton John and the piano. This was my first indoor venue, and the noise was incredible. Again, the details of the show have faded with time, but I remember the feeling of the music—the drums, guitars, piano—along with the crowd creating energy throughout the enclosed arena. Such an amazing experience. If my first concert experience wasn't enough to get me hooked on seeing Elton John live, this concert certainly was!

After that second show, I was convinced that going to Elton John concerts was going to be my thing. Once again, my excitement overruled my common sense, in that I never factored in the amount of money this new hobby/passion/thing would cost. Looking back on it now, it was just downright foolish for me to choose going to see Elton John live as the thing I wanted to spend my life doing. At the time, I was a college student with little to no income from a middle-class family that had two more kids to put through college. Sure, I suppose I could have quit school, gotten a full-time job, and spend as much time as possible being an Elton groupie, but that wasn't an option. It was expected at that time that I would not only attend college, but finish in four years, graduate, and land a job.

I went to college to get a degree in biology because all I ever wanted to do was be a veterinarian. I maintained that idea until my first semester of my sophomore year, when I was sitting in biology class and just had a feeling that things weren't right. That being a veterinarian wasn't what I wanted to do. I didn't know what else I wanted to do—I just knew that this wasn't it. I dropped the class and had to reconsider my whole life; I mean, what else did I want to do? What else was I interested in? I truly did not know. Everything I had done educationally leading up to this point was focused on one career option.

I had to declare a major, and I needed to do it soon so my class schedule could reflect my major. They had a Liberal Arts major at my school, so I chose that. What was I going to do with a Liberal Arts degree? I had no idea.

At the beginning of my sophomore year, I pledged a co-ed fraternity called Alpha Phi Omega. We were a service-based fraternity, and that particular year, we volunteered to help kids participating in the Special Olympics on our campus. I was paired up with a young boy in a wheelchair (I believe he had cerebral palsy). My job was basically to encourage him as he participated. I wasn't too sure about it at first, but I ended up having an absolute blast. After the event was over, I realized I'd had a great time volunteering at the entire event and being around kids with disabilities. I had an idea—one, of course, that would totally financially support my big dream of seeing Elton John in concert as often as I possibly could. I decided to major in Special Education and become a teacher.

Of course, choosing this option made no sense whatsoever, especially from a financial aspect. I knew that teachers made a very low salary since my mom was a teacher. I knew when I chose this career option that I would most likely not ever make enough money to pursue my dream the way I wanted to. But I chose it anyway, because I loved working with those kids. I believed a career working with students who had disabilities was the career I was called by God to do.

Looking back on it now, I guess I assumed that something would work out financially. When you have a dream or you pursue a passion, common sense doesn't factor into the equation. I believe that's why it's called a dream.

Life Lesson:
Find a job that fits your passion.
The money will follow.

5
<u>Adulting</u>

As I transitioned from graduating college to starting my life as a real adult with a real job and real bills, I found myself having to evaluate just how important this dream was to me. Of course, knowing that going to see Elton John in concert was going to cost money, you'd think I would major in and choose the profession that would earn me the most money possible to pursue this passion. But I became a teacher.

I got my first taste of what this dream was going to cost, in terms of non-monetary resources like time and sleep, when I attended my third concert, this time in Columbia, South Carolina. It was the first show I would see with Elton John and Billy Joel together, called the Face to Face tour. I went with friends for the almost two-hour drive there and back (it's important to note here that my friends were more excited to see Billy Joel than they were Elton John).

As a senior in college, I worked to help pay my way through. I almost didn't return for my senior year because the summer before, my dad unexpectedly lost his job. Not only did he lose his job; he lost his career. Gone were the days when you could work for one company your entire career and retire early. This event came as quite a shock to our entire family. My parents had two kids in college and another starting soon. It took a lot of hard conversations and yes, obtaining student loans, but everything worked out for me to finish my last year of school.

At this point, it would be my last year because I had changed majors and decided to go right into teaching after graduation. Although I wasn't fully financially supporting myself, there wasn't a whole lot of extra money, so when we went to Columbia for the show, my friends and I sat in the nosebleed seats in the football stadium where the concert was held.

The show was awesome anyway, as my two favorite piano-playing musicians faced each other with their gleaming black pianos and wowed the crowd with their set list. Elton John had his set list, Billy Joel had his, and then they took turns singing each other's songs and added a few duets.

The concert didn't end until almost 11:00 that night, and we had an almost two-hour drive back to school. Normally, that would have been fine if we could *just this once* ~~sleep through~~ skip class, but as an education major, I was to begin my student teaching assignment the following morning.

Coming in late from attending a concert and then having to get up early to begin student teaching was not exactly a great way to start a process that is vital to obtaining my teaching degree. Sometimes, when you are pursuing a dream, these decisions must be made. This would be one of many important lessons I learned about pursuing a dream.

Another lesson I learned from attending this show is to never again buy tickets in the nosebleed section of a venue. I am certain the price was right for my meager college student budget, but by this time, I was no longer satisfied with just being in the same space as Elton John. I wanted to be close to him. This was only my third concert, and the closest seat I'd had was that front-row balcony seat overlooking the stage. My goal of attaining a front-row seat become stronger the further away my seat was for the show. The closer the seat, the more time I would spend visualizing myself in that front-row seat.

At this point, I was starting to formulate priorities in pursuing the dream. I realized that time wasn't exactly on my side, and a sense of urgency was beginning to emerge. It was no longer good enough just to be there. The more I pursued the dream, the more the passion to make it come true started to take root. The more the passion took root, the more I wanted to share my passion for having a dream with others.

Life Lesson:
Don't let life get in the way of pursuing the dream.
Adult responsibilities need not deter the pursuit.

6
__Perspective__

In May 1995, I graduated from college and, shortly thereafter, accepted a teaching position at a high school in Lincolnton, North Carolina. I would be teaching freshman who had learning disabilities. As my passion for achieving a dream was just beginning to grow, I wanted to instill the same "get a dream and chase after it" ideal into the young minds of my students.

Little did I know at the time that they were just trying to survive the day-to-day life of being a teenager in a town where most people never traveled far. Like, ever. Most of my students came from generations of families who never left town. It was fascinating to them that not only had I left home to attend college, but that I had attended college. I remember having whole conversations with them about how I lived in one town and my family lived in another, three hours away. They couldn't wrap their minds around why I would ever leave "home," and I couldn't understand why they had no desire to travel outside of their own town. It's just the way their lives were.

It was an interesting perspective for me because I grew up in a family that always traveled. Mostly, we'd go see family who had moved to another state, but we always traveled. I suppose it never occurred to me that there were people who never did. But, there were. They were my students. My high school kids—who had never experienced loading up the minivan with everything needed for a week-long trip, having to ride in that minivan with parents, brothers, and sisters for hours on end—had, shockingly, never uttered the words, "Are we there yet?"

So, there I was, a new teacher with a fairly new, grandiose dream of meeting Elton John—who most of my students had never heard of—and I was with a group of kids who had never even thought about leaving the town they grew up in.

I quickly learned that not everyone has been taught to dream outside the box, per se. Was it my job to teach them this? Not necessarily; not every family wants their kids to leave home and explore the world. There's a fine line between encouraging kids to follow their dreams and planting ideas in their head. There's also a line between what I want to talk about with my students and what their parents want them to know about. (Keep in mind, this was the mid-90s, and there was still a very deep divide of opinions between accepting gays and being against the lifestyle. Add to this that I was teaching in the Bible Belt—and not just the Bible Belt, but an area of North Carolina that was deeply rooted in religion. A religion that followed the teachings of the Bible to the letter of the law.)

I was raised in a traditional Irish-Italian Roman Catholic family—generations of Roman Catholics. We were raised to follow all the teaching of the Roman Catholic faith. However, teaching in the Bible Belt is much different than living out the tenants of the Roman Catholic faith. We all believe in God, but there are different teachings based on the different religious denominations.

It was in the mid-80s when Elton John developed a relationship with Ryan White. After Ryan's death, Elton John created the Elton John AIDS Foundation. Certainly, by the mid-90s, it was well documented that Elton John was gay. So, to some, being such a huge fan meant that I automatically accepted his lifestyle, and that was not acceptable to many people. Did I automatically accept the lifestyle? Not at first. I had a very clear stance of loving Elton's music, but not necessarily who he was as a person. At the time, I didn't think I could defend my faith against his lifestyle.

What was clear to me, however, was not clear to others. There was a perception that if I loved Elton's music, then I also accepted him as a person, which included his lifestyle. I had to learn to answer the hard questions, which I mostly did by avoiding them. I had to accept that some people made the conclusion that by my accepting Elton and his lifestyle, I also, perhaps, lived a similar lifestyle.

It was an easy conclusion to make. I was not a girly-girl in any way. I was a tomboy, tried and true. I didn't have a serious boyfriend. I sporadically went out on dates. I had graduated from college, started a career, and lived alone with my dog.

I could see how people could make assumptions. I had not followed the "go to college, find a nice guy, and get married" track of life that so many people expected. I was content, then, to focus on my career teaching high school kids. I wanted so desperately to teach them more than what was expected of me in the standard course of study.

Over time, I learned that I can just be and do, and they will observe. I can teach more by showing than talking. It's not just enough for me to use my position as a teacher to tell the kids to follow their dreams—I had to show them I was following mine.

Life Lesson:

When presented with conflict in the pursuit of your dream, don't let the conflict win. Pursue your dream above all else.

7
Leaving the Comfort Zone

You've probably heard the saying, "It's not what you know, it's who you know." By this point in my journey, I already knew how to find out Elton's tour schedule, buy tickets, and get my friends to come with me. I was at the point at which I always bought two tickets to every show, and then asked someone to go with me. You would think it might be easy to get someone to go to a free concert, but it's not, really. Not everyone was as excited to go see Elton John as I was, which, to this day, I still have a hard time understanding.

In February 1999, I prepared to attend my ninth Elton John show. This time, I would make the trip from Charlotte, North Carolina, to Roanoke, Virginia. This concert tour was the first of many solo shows featuring just Elton and his piano. While I do have a great appreciation for the band, it was my chance to see my two favorite things: Elton and his piano.

Seriously, you know an artist is good when a venue is filled to only see those two things. This show was the first in the tour. My concert program has the following quote on it:

> *"You need to go back and be scared once in a while…it's very rewarding to do shows on your own; it gives you a chance to talk to the audience."*

So, what does it mean to do things *scared*? Well, it means stepping outside of your comfort zone. It means doing things you wouldn't normally do, standing out on your own, talking to the audience.

This was the first time I had a seat on the floor, which is an outstanding place to be because it's closer to the stage. However, little did I know at the time that if you sit in the second section of the floor, you can't get anywhere near the stage. This seat would turn out to be a particularly important one, as it gave me access to meet someone who would have an impact on my journey.

As we were standing near our seats, I scanned down toward the stage and saw her standing there. I recognized her, but I couldn't immediately remember how or why. Then I remembered I had seen her before; in fact, eight times before. Like, at all the other shows I attended. She was always in the front row, near the stage—exactly where I wanted to be! I had to meet her. So, I told my cousin who was with me that I'd be right back, and took off toward her.

The usher in between sections stopped me and asked to see my ticket. I wasn't sure why she wanted to see it, but I handed it to her anyway. She looked at it and said, "Oh! Your seat is behind you."

"Yes," I replied, "I just came from there. I am going to see my…*friend* who is standing up there."

"I'm sorry," said the usher, "you can't go up there; your ticket does not allow you access." Since my seat wasn't in her section, I couldn't go in her section.

Stupid ticket rules. Thinking on my feet, I asked the usher, "You see that girl standing by the stage, who sort of looks like me—but her hair is a little longer and she's a bit taller?"

"Yes," she replied.

"Can you go get her for me? I need to talk to her."

To my surprise, the usher complied and walked down the aisle toward my *friend*. When she turned, and looked at me, I just started waving at her like we were long-lost friends.

To my surprise, she started walking toward me.

In our brief conversation, I told her how I had seen her before, how this was my ninth show, I was so happy to be there, etc., and we exchanged contact information.

I emailed her when I got home, and we became electronic pen pals. Turns out, she worked for a radio station and had been a fan of Elton for much longer than I had. For years after this meeting, Valerie and I traveled together to attend concerts. She would be the single most important catalyst for many of the grand adventures that would ensue. I learned more from her about "chasing Elton" than anyone else to that point. Through her, I learned closely-guarded and valuable information that, when utilized properly, got me closer and closer to achieving my dream.

Over time, I, too, became wise to the ways of avid fans and developed the adage of, "It's what you know *and* who you know."

Life Lessons:

1. *Stand Out.*
   Valerie always wore black to concerts and an "E" and "J" on her lapel. That is one of the reasons I recognized her.

2. *Think on your feet and trust your brain.*
   I had a plan to meet Valerie, but that plan didn't work out the way I had intended. I had to think fast to get past the usher.

3. *Have an idea and stick to it.*
   Once you have an idea, push through the obstacles. If I had just returned to my seat after being denied access to Valerie's section, I would not have met her.

8
The Big Picture

People are interesting. They can either totally stand in the way of you achieving your dream, or they can help you get there. I have learned it all depends on what you allow to happen.

When I got my first car in 1996, I decided I wanted a personalized license plate for no other reason than because I could. After several attempts to combine what I loved into an eight-letter word that made sense to the drivers behind me, I finally settled on RKTMNFAN.

Sometimes, people would figure it out. Other times, they wouldn't, and when I would tell them it means, "Rocket Man Fan," I often got a blank stare in return.

"Who sings *Rocket Man*?" I would ask.

"Um, um...oh, I know that song!" would be the reply.

Eventually, they would come up with Elton John, or else I would tell them. I would then have to further explain that that is my favorite song by my favorite artist.

Nothing dings your dream more than getting blank stares from people when you tell them your life-long dream is to meet Elton John. Or that Elton John is your favorite musician. Especially as a single, female young adult. People made fun of me and thought it was odd. But by this point, I was used to it. It didn't make it any easier, but at least I knew to expect it from people.

But then again, people used to say, and still do, the same about Elton—and by this time, I knew enough of his history to not let it bother me. One very important lesson my journey up to this point had taught me was, don't give a crap what other people think of your dream.

Many times, I had a thought to change that license plate. Just get a normal one, like normal people. Many times, I talked myself into it, and then just as many more times, I didn't go through with it. Talking about doing something and doing it are two entirely different things. In this case, I'm glad I didn't let others dictate for me what kind of license plate I wanted on my car. Over the years, my plate would change, but it would always be some variation of "Rocket Man Fan."

The second plate I had was RCKTMNFN, and the third one I had was RKTMNFN2. Currently, it's back to the original RKTMNFAN, because by some stroke of luck, it became available again.

Here's the important thing about publicly announcing your dream: it becomes a part of your identity. That plate, regardless of what car I'm driving, has become the identifying factor of *that's Melissa's car*. It has, in more ways than one, helped me meet the people who would open doors for me in the pursuit of my dream. That one piece of metal with eight letters would be a small part in the bigger picture of my journey.

Over time, due to circumstances a bit out of our control, Valerie and I lost touch with each other. It would come to pass that she changed jobs and I moved, and we just simply had no other way to contact each other.

Life Lesson:
Not everyone will be as excited about your dream as you are; pursue it anyway.
*Make your dream part of your identity. Your dream is **yours**.*

44

9
The One

Meeting Valerie in 1999 was a highlight of the year, but an even greater life event happened around that same time: I met my husband. Of course, I didn't know when we first met that he would be the One, but after six hours of chatting in an online chat box, I had a pretty good idea.

The time had come for me to share my life with someone, and I wasn't getting anywhere using traditional methods: going to college, being set up by friends, or just some chance serendipitous meeting. I was well into my career as a special education teacher, I had my own apartment, and my circle of friends was well established. I loved living the single life, but I also felt like it was time to find someone to share it with.

Here I was, a Catholic school teacher who loved Elton John and my dogs. I had a sense that I knew what I was looking for in a guy, and I was fiercely independent. I wanted to share my life, not have someone come in and control it for me. My friend and I signed up for a local dating service and, for me, many guys did not make it past the first phone call, let alone the first date.

There always seemed to be something that wasn't quite right. I didn't give guys a chance at a second date if I didn't feel like the first one went very well. I was picky, picky, picky!

It was a frustrating process.

One night in December of 1999, I came home from a date—that I knew would not turn into a second date—so frustrated that I slammed my apartment door shut, pointed up to the sky, and yelled, "Fine! You do it, because I am done!" (Yes, even as a born and practicing Catholic, my prayer life at that point mostly consisted of me yelling at God.)

I made a choice, right then and there, that I was going on a dating break. I put an "unavailable" notice on my dating service profile, and I was not going to respond or pursue until after the first of the year.

I also had a profile on AOL.com. I think it was called Love@ AOL. Online dating was a new thing in late 1999, and AOL was the popular Internet service at the time, so I thought it was a good idea to put a dating profile there. I did meet some guys through this service, and was always careful to meet them at a busy restaurant or public place. On some occasions, my neighbors would "show up" at the restaurant where I was with my date. I even had a pager and would have a friend call it about halfway through a date so I could return the call and, if needed, leave early.

I happened to be at my parents' house the week of Christmas, and one evening, while chatting online with friends though AOL, I saw a new message pop up.

Hello?

Oh, no, I thought. *Who is that?*

A quick profile check let me know that it was a guy who had seen my AOL profile and was messaging me. But I was on a break, so I didn't know how to respond.

I wrote back, *Hello.*

He responded, *How are you?*

I responded, *Fine.*

I was hoping if I responded in one-word answers that he would go away. He didn't, and six hours later, we were still chatting online. I later found out his side of the story.

As an active duty Marine, Jack was stationed on the U.S.S.

Bataan and was in the middle of the Mediterranean Sea when he met me online. (I suppose that's why I continued an online conversation with him; he wasn't going to initiate seeing me anytime soon, and he was halfway across the world.) He ended his shift and was walking back to the bunk area when he saw one of his shipmates scrolling through pictures online. Jack asked what he was doing, and the shipmate explained the process of looking through pictures, then messaging someone he would like to get to know better. As the shipmate was scrolling, Jack saw my picture and read my profile. He then sat down at the adjoining computer and sent me that now-infamous first *Hello?* message.

Our online conversation ended because he had to go back to work. He'd been chatting with me when he was supposed to be sleeping. Of course, I didn't know this and felt horrible about it, but I was also excited to get to know this guy better, so we agreed to keep in touch via chat and email.

By the time he was preparing to return to the States, we'd had several conversations via email and chat, many of those being important relationship questions—and it seemed that we were very compatible (online, anyway). We agreed that when we met in person, if we could stand to be in the same room with each other, we should date because the online relationship was going so well.

We finally met in person in February of 2000. It was just before Valentine's Day, and although we had previously agreed to not meet until after Valentine's Day, he had another plan (well, his commanding officer had another plan). When they arrived back at Camp Lejeune, North Carolina, Jack was pretty much given "orders" to drive to Charlotte to meet me. He arrived on a Thursday night around 9:00 and called me. I was surprised to hear from him, since I wasn't sure when he was returning to

North Carolina and I was already in bed for the night. At some point, I asked him if he'd found an apartment or new living arrangements yet, and he replied that he was at a hotel.

"Why are you there? I asked.

"Because I'm in Charlotte," he responded.

What? How can that be? I thought he was at Camp Lejeune. I was so confused and unsure if I believed him, so I said, "Look out your window; tell me what you see."

"I'm near a mall and I see…" and he rattled of a list of stores I knew were at that mall.

I knew exactly where he was: at a hotel about five miles from my apartment. He was, indeed, in Charlotte. I was not prepared to meet him and was genuinely surprised. I didn't know what to do, so I panicked.

"Uh, ok. I have to go walk the dog; can I call you back?"

"Yes," he replied. I hung up the phone.

I looked up the number for the hotel and called.

"Hello, do you have a Jack Thomas registered at your hotel?"

"Yes," the desk clerk answered. "Would you like me to transfer you?"

"No, no, that's fine," I said. "Thank you."

Now what would I do? I wanted to go meet him, but by the time I showered and changed and drove over there, it would be late, and I had to go to work in the morning. I called my friend who knew we had met online and told her what happened.

She said, "Why are you calling me? Get dressed. Put on jeans and a t-shirt and a baseball hat and go meet him! Call me when you get there and call me when you get home."

"Okay," I answered, and did just that. I got dressed and drove over to the hotel. I called him from the lobby and told him I was there. He said he would come to the lobby to meet me. I couldn't believe this was happening. *This is crazy! I don't do these crazy things! I'm meeting some random online guy in the lobby of a hotel at 10:00 at night.*

It didn't occur to me to bail on my idea at this point, so I found a couch to sit on facing the stairway where I thought he would come down. I could see the entire lobby and the front desk clerk. Then, I heard a door close behind me, and I just knew it was him.

"Are you Melissa?"

I turned around to see him standing before me.

I answered, "Yes, and this is what you get for surprising me. I just threw on this outfit and came over to meet you."

An awkward silence followed because we didn't know what to do; after all, we knew each other, but we hadn't ever actually met. *Do we shake hands like a formal introduction? That seems weird. Do we hug like long-lost friends? That seems weird, too.*

Jack eventually broke through the awkwardness and asked, "Would it be okay if I gave you a hug?"

I agreed, and we embraced. I knew at that moment, standing in the lobby of the hotel, that he was indeed *The One.* I know, without a doubt, God hand-picked Jack just for me. There is no other explanation for it. Chances are, we never would have met in our social circles or through mutual friends.

When I met Jack online, I told him of my love for Elton John and my big dream to meet him. I'm sure he thought this was weird, but the difference between him and other guys was that he supported it. It's important to discuss your dreams with the ones you love. Let the people in your inner circle know what it's all about, why you want to do it, and they can either support it (which is your preference) or not. It's up to you to draw the proverbial line in the sand on whether you will continue to have them in your life if they choose to not support you.

People often ask me, "What does Jack think of you going

to see Elton all the time?" Well, Jack thinks it's great. He has known since he met me that I was a huge fan, that going to see Elton was my thing. At some point, I shared with him the dream to meet Elton one day. It's not exactly first date conversation, but the first time he came over to my apartment, he'd get clued in.

The poster from my very first concert that I'd bought and framed was hanging on the wall of the living room in my apartment. Anyone who came over saw it. It was actually hard to miss. I'm sure I talked about my concert experiences in conversation as well. But it wasn't overwhelming. It's not like I listened to Elton's music 24/7 or talked about him incessantly.

I am not some crazy stalker. No, I am just a person with a passion, a dream. I also had a life that my dream was a part of; not a dream that my life fit into. There is a difference. Every decision I made as an adult always considered one factor—going to see Elton John. But I had a job, friends, and other hobbies and interests. I was a well-rounded person.

I had church, work, my dogs, my friends, and my family. I went out, played softball, and spent time with family. Life was good. My life did not consume my dream, and my dream did not consume my life. It was possible for me to go out in society and talk about other things than that which pertained to all things Elton. But, if the company at hand was interested, I could also talk for hours on end about every concert experience or new album or song.

My inner circle of people helped to make up the Big Picture. God knew what I needed in Jack as a partner: not only someone who loved me for who I am, but someone who had absolutely no desire to ever attend an Elton John concert.

We were engaged within five months of meeting in person, and married ten months after that. On May 5, 2017, we celebrated our sixteenth wedding anniversary. I've been to twenty-six

Elton John concerts since Jack came into my life, and he has not attended one!

Life Lesson:

Give your struggles and frustrations to God, and be sure everyone who is in your boat is helping you row, not trying to throw out the anchor along the way.

10
Someday, Out of the Blue

One month after we were married in June 2001, Jack and I moved to Wilmington, North Carolina—me from Charlotte, North Carolina, and Jack from Jacksonville, North Carolina. We were finally together in the same city. One day, we were driving down a main road in Wilmington in my car with my RKTMNFAN license plate. As we were sitting at the stoplight, Jack said, "I think that person next to us is trying to get your attention."

I looked over and indeed, there was a lady in the car doing just that. Jack rolled down the window and she yelled, "Does your license plate say, 'Rocket Man Fan,' as in, Elton John?"

"Yes! Yes!" I replied.

"Oh, wow! I'm a huge fan, too!" she exclaimed. "Quick, give me your contact info!"

I had nothing, so she handed a piece of paper through the open window. Written on it was her email address. The light turned green and we drove our separate ways. As she drove away, I looked at my husband and said, "She understood my license plate! I must email her as soon as I get home!" Jack just looked over and smiled at me. He knew how much this little moment excited me. (I am so blessed to have met a man who supports me and all my crazy adventures.)

I could not wait to get home and send out an email to my new traffic light friend. This was before smartphones, so I had no other choice but to wait. I put that little scrap of paper in my pocket for safekeeping.

My email to her went something like this:

Hi! This is Melissa. We met at the traffic light at 17th street. My license plate is RKTMNFAN. I'm SO excited that you knew what that meant, and it's always great to meet another fan! I look forward to hearing back from you soon!

To my surprise, I realized she was Valerie! Only God could have orchestrated that chance meeting. That makes two times that Valerie was brought into my life. And even though the first time I sort of initiated it, I firmly believe the idea to formulate a plan to go meet her was not my own. I usually didn't do things like that at the time. That's not to say I didn't have crazy ideas; I just didn't pursue them, and certainly didn't persevere through challenges. I just knew there was a reason for running into each other at the traffic light. Little did I know at the time how much of a role Valerie would play in the pursuit of my dream.

Life Lesson:

Follow Up!
If someone shares their contact information with you, follow up with them. It might not lead anywhere, but it might. And where it leads just might change your life.

11
Look Out, New World

Valerie and I shared so many exciting adventures after reconnecting at the traffic light. For one thing, we made sure to always stay in touch with each other. We make a great traveling team and always had a grand adventure. The first of these adventures started with a simple phone call.

It was late at night when she called. "Someone has a ninth-row ticket for sale for the Norfolk concert. You better go get it!"

I had never purchased a ticket other than through Ticketmaster, so I was a bit hesitant. I decided to buy it anyway—had to take that chance to sit in the ninth row! This would be my eleventh concert, and I had never been that close.

Upon arrival at Norfolk, I met up with the guy who was selling the ticket. He had two, and whoever was supposed to join him that day couldn't go. I was indeed in the ninth row. I'd kept my other ticket just in case this ninth-row situation was a scam; there was no way I was going all the way to Norfolk to not have a ticket. So, yes, I bought two tickets and only used one, but it was worth it.

It's quite a difference going from that first concert about forty rows back to sitting on the ninth row. Nine rows from the stage meant I was close enough to see everything on stage without binoculars. Nine rows from the stage meant my vision from that first concert of sitting in the front row came that much closer to being a reality. Sitting on the ninth row gave me a new perspective, a new determination to pursue my dream of meeting Elton John. To this point, I had been to eleven concerts, so I was well into the mindset of attending as many as possible, regardless of where I had to go. Little did I know how making the decision to buy that ninth-row ticket would lead me to expand my travels beyond the borders of surrounding states. I was about to enter a new world of traveling that started with a trip to the Big City.

In my mind, there is only one Big City, and that is New York City. I grew up in upstate New York and remember taking trips to the Big City as a child. I was excited to find out Elton would be performing at Radio City Music Hall in July of 2004. I offered my sister the opportunity to travel with me and attend the concert. This was my twelfth concert, but her first, and I was excited to share the experience.

We traveled from North Carolina to New York City by plane and stayed with our aunt in Long Beach. It was just a train ride into the city from her house, and from the train we could take the subway or other transportation. I remember one subway ride, in particular: the ride from Penn Station to the 9/11 Memorial. Remember, this was 2004, only three years after 9/11. My sister and I decided to take some time to visit the site while we were in the area. I remember getting off the subway at the Memorial site and commenting to my sister, "Wow, this is all brand new."

It was distinctly all brand new; everything was super clean and bright white, and it just felt new; it smelled new. When I looked at my sister, she was just staring at me, dumbfounded that I had made such a statement out loud. Then, it hit me: *Of course, it's all brand new. This station was damaged when the buildings collapsed.* The gravity of standing there in that moment hit me like the proverbial ton of bricks. It was brand new because it had been destroyed.

It's one thing to watch the buildings collapse on television and read the news reports in the aftermath. It's an entirely different experience to stand in a subway station that has been rebuilt because of that event. It was surreal, and certainly felt like I was standing on and about to enter hallowed ground.

At this point, the entire World Trade Center site was surrounded by chain link fencing and we couldn't get very close to the site. There were mementos, pictures, and flowers stuck in the fence, along with posters of people still missing. My heart broke as I walked along the fence and saw so many reminders of that awful day. Looking through the fence, all I could see was a bottomless hole of dirt. I couldn't imagine that two powerful skyscrapers once occupied that spot. The silence of the area was eerie and, emotionally, it was a difficult space to be in. It was, indeed, a new world we lived in after 9/11. I gained great perspective.

The purpose of this trip, however, was not to visit that site. It was to visit a New York City icon—Radio City Music Hall— to see Elton John. We had seats in the upper balcony, which is a distance from the ninth row of the previous concert, but I was still glad to be there. I was inside Radio City Music Hall attending another concert, and this was my first long-distance trip to see Elton John. Nothing says, "I'm committed to pursuing a dream," like getting on an airplane to attend a concert. This trip opened my eyes to the world of traveling, and another Elton John show was the perfect excuse.

Life Lesson:
Take advantage of opportunities, both those that take you closer to your dream and those that give you opportunity to explore and open up a new world.

12
The Turning Point

Several months prior to March 2007, Valerie contacted me about a significant concert event. Elton John was going to celebrate his sixtieth birthday with a concert at Madison Square Garden in New York City. This was also to be his sixtieth concert performed at that magical venue. This is what's known as a once-in-a-lifetime experience.

By this time, I was a stay-at-home mom working with a direct sales company. Jack and I had two sons, ages two and one. We were already accustomed to the paycheck-to-paycheck financial lifestyle. My work with the direct sales company was good, but not bringing in a lot of money; mostly just enough to cover my business expenses. It was more of a hobby that an actual income producer. This concert would be my fifteenth Elton John concert, and such a thrill to be part of this once-in-a-lifetime experience.

Yes, it would have been.

I didn't go. I couldn't. We did not have the money. This trip would have been a flight, a hotel in New York City, and the concert ticket, which was way more than normal, given the occasion. A lifetime of bad money habits had finally caught up to me. Normally, I would have gone and put the trip on a credit card, but I couldn't do that with credit cards that were almost maxed out. I couldn't take the risk of spending that money on a concert trip, and then not having the money available for an emergency. Looking back, I could have sold some things and earned money for the trip, but I didn't think like that back then.

I wanted to go, but I could not. Money was the one thing that stood in the way.

"What do you mean you are not going? You are Elton's biggest fan!"

"I…I just can't go," I answered, making up any excuse that didn't relate to money. It was too embarrassing to explain I didn't have the money to go. After all, we live in a society where if we want something, we get it. That's what credit cards are for, right?

At the time, that was my mindset, too, but if there is not enough money on the credit card, then there just isn't any money. Valerie was going to this concert, and oh, how she tried and tried to get me to go! I'm sure we spent time on the phone trying to figure out a way, but it just wasn't happening. The amount of money I needed to spend was not there, and it wasn't just going to magically appear in the timeframe that I needed it.

There was plenty of media coverage for this event. I felt sad that I was not able to be there. I couldn't understand how I had gotten myself into this financial situation. What happened to me?

Certainly, I knew better. Financial management isn't rocket science, but it is something you must do: manage. Managing money means living below your means. We were not doing that. We had the same mindset as everyone we knew. The banks gave us a loan and we got approved for another credit card, so they must think we can afford the payments. We had a mortgage and two car payments for brand new cars that we purchased in 2003 and 2005, respectively.

Our biggest financial mistake, however, wasn't taking on more loans then we could manage. It was actually a series of events that got us to this point. In October 2003, we bought a new car for me. Also around that time, Jack retired from the United States Marine Corps. He accepted a job working at Duke Energy in Southport, North Carolina, so we set a plan to buy a house there.

We had no financial business buying a house at all. Our first clue was that we were denied a mortgage by the bank and had to go to a mortgage broker. She helped us secure a mortgage at a higher rate, but we got the mortgage. In January 2005, we bought Jack a new truck, so now we had a house payment, a car payment, and a truck payment. Six months later, our first son was born. By default, I became a stay-at-home mom. My retail job at the time was paying me just enough to cover daycare expenses, so it didn't make sense to pay for daycare. I liked that job, but I didn't love it enough to sign an entire paycheck over for childcare. It seemed "the thing" to be a stay-at-home mom, so that's what I did. We quickly went from a two-income family to a one-income family, and yet we never changed our financial lifestyle. We did what everyone else did: used a credit card or two (or three) when we ran out of money before we ran out of month.

Our second son was born in 2006. Mortgage. Two car payments. Two kids. One income. No clue of the financial disaster that lay ahead of us.

Looking back now, I'm not even sure how I managed that aspect of our lives. I do remember times when I used one credit card to make a minimum payment on another. I don't think it occurred to us to trade in our almost-new cars for less expensive, new-to-us cars. If it did, we certainly abashed the idea, because that was crazy. Doing that would lead others to believe we were having money problems, and we weren't going to let that happen. You don't sell cars if you're financially set. No one did that. Why should we?

It certainly never occurred to us to sell the house and downsize. We had a three bedroom, two bath house. It was just right for our family. But not really. It was, but it wasn't. We wanted a bigger living room and a playroom for the boys.

At the time, our living room was the family room/TV room/ boys' playroom, and every day looked like I ran a daycare center out of our home. It was easier to put an addition on the house than it was to move, so that's what we did. We took out a home equity loan. We were getting ready to start a massive renovation project to put a five-hundred-square-foot addition on our house. We already had a mortgage, two vehicle loans, credit card debt, and now we were taking out another loan. But it was okay; the bank approved us, so we must be able to make the payment, right?

All those factors prevented me from pursuing my dream. Would I have met Elton John at that sixtieth birthday concert? Probably not, but I would have at least been there. As a fan, I would have thoroughly loved every minute of the experience. I was embarrassed to tell people I couldn't go, and it was worse when the concert was made available online. I watched it but didn't enjoy it, because all I kept thinking was that I should have been there.

I felt worse when Valerie returned home from the concert and told me all about her experience. I went from feeling sad to feeling angry. Not at Valerie, but at myself. I should have been there. I should have managed my money better. This experience taught me it's one thing to have people make fun of you because of your dream; it's another to pursue it, have everyone know about it, and then tell them you can't attend a once-in-a-lifetime event.

This was a huge turning point for me in dealing with personal finances. I made the vow right then and there that I was no longer going to let money stand in my way of going to see Elton John. I needed a better plan.

Life Lesson:
Don't let money stand in the way of pursuing your dream.

13
Problem Solving, Part 1

Once I made that decision, I created a plan. I was going to step it up in my direct sales business. I spoke to my leader and we created a plan to increase income. One of the basic tenets of success in a direct sales company is to find someone in my upline who is successful, and then copy their steps to success. That's the benefit of a direct sales company; everyone starts at the bottom and follows a proven process to success.

I had an added incentive to success: the ability to earn an all-expense-paid cruise on Carnival Cruise Lines. It was the thirtieth anniversary of the company and they were offering the opportunity to earn the trip of a lifetime. As a bonus, the entire ship was reserved just for our company. It would happen in May of 2008, which is also the month or our wedding anniversary. I was all in. I was excited about going on a cruise for the first time and excited to earn a free vacation for my husband and me.

For months, I worked extra hard to book parties and sell products. I also had to build a team, which is the way to financial success with direct sales. I threw myself into learning all I could about how to run a business, not just a hobby job. I attended seminars, both locally and out of town. I was on conference calls, and I met other consultants and learned from them. I had a plan with specific and measurable goals, and I knew what I needed to do to earn each step of the process toward earning the trip.

With all this personal development, the most important thing

I learned was to learn from others. How were others successful? How did they do it? Was it a process I could follow? The most common theme among the successful people was that they always asked. They asked for the party, they asked for the sale, they asked and asked and asked again.

So, I did what they did: I asked. I asked people to host parties, buy product, and be on my team. I taught them what I had learned, took them with me to meetings, and made sure they were on conference calls.

I did, indeed, make more money, and I earned that trip. From May 18-25, 2008, we were on vacation traveling the high seas, with stops in Nassau, Bahamas, Grand Cayman, and Cozumel, Mexico. We toured Atlantis Resort and swam with stingrays. We had a fantastic time, but one thing hadn't changed: we still weren't ahead with our finances.

Yes, I was earning consistent income and receiving bonuses as I built my team, but I still wasn't managing it well. We didn't have a financial plan—no budget, no savings plan, no idea what our long- and short-term financial goals were. I was, however, making enough money to go to more Elton John concerts, and for that, I was happy. Since missing out on that March 2007 concert, I have been to every Elton John concert that I could attend. Money no longer became an obstacle to my dream.

Life Lesson:
If you don't ask, the answer is always no.

14
Persistence and Perseverance

The experience of not being able to attend the sixtieth birthday concert changed me in more ways than one. I knew I needed a better financial plan, but I also knew deep down in my soul that this experience of attending concerts and pursuing my dream to meet Elton John is absolutely one my life's purposes. I shifted the mindset from setting a goal and attaining it to developing an attitude of not letting anything stand in my way. I attended my fourteenth concert shortly after the infamous sixtieth birthday party concert. This is the email summary I sent out to friends and family afterward: (it is added here in its original form)

May 4, 2007
Greenville, SC
I drove for seven hours the same day as the concert just to see him, the excitement of the evening and several cups of coffee keeping me going. Once in Asheville, I arrived at the house of my cousin Sean and his wife, Julie who were joining me for the big event. A little time to visit, a quick change of clothes and we were off to dinner. So, it was back in the car and another hour of driving. Once we got to the Bi-Lo Center, I saw the semi-trucks that haul the band's equipment and immediately, the butterflies started in my stomach. As we approached the doors, there was already a line to get it. All these people here just to see him – I am always amazed. I find myself looking around, taking in all the sights of the people, the sounds of his music playing over the

remote trucks of the local radio stations. The butterflies in my stomach are really going now, the excitement builds.

As we move forward in the line, I notice that people are being wanded for weapons and bags are being searched. The guy who is to wand me says, very bluntly, "you can't bring that in with you." (referring to my RCKTMNFN license plate). I stare at him in disbelief and ask why. He says I can't bring in gifts for Elton. I try to explain but at first, he doesn't want to listen, he just wants me to take the plate back to the car. No way I am going into that arena without my plate! My heart is racing; my pulse pounding and I feel my Irish temper started to rear its ugly head. So, I bristle up a bit and without being disrespectful, just tell him that it is MY plate, not a gift for Elton and I am taking it in. He concedes and the incident is over.

My ticket is scanned, I am in the arena and I have my plate with me! I decide to make a stop at the merchandise kiosk and strike up a conversation with a father and son in line behind me. It was the sons' first concert. He was a teenager and so excited to be seeing Elton. I show off my twice-autographed plate and we chat a bit about our favorite songs etc. Soon, it is my turn to purchase a souvenir and I decide that while I would really LOVE to have the $400 leather jacket, I better just buy the $25 program instead. Julie buys a Goodbye Yellow Brick Road coffee mug and we are off to our seats.

We go through the entrance marked "Floor seats" and I pause at the top of the stairs, my eyes find the stage. There it is, HIS piano, the black gloss gleaming in the light. We descend the steps and I have that surreal feeling that I can't believe I am finally here. Once on the floor, we make a quick lap around the front row looking for Julie's friend who got SECOND row seats the morning of the show!!! I avoid the temptation to jump up on the stage and touch the piano for while I am only a few feet away *from it, I am certain I would have been escorted out.*

Once in our seats, I find myself scouting out the scene and trying to figure out how I am going to get up to the stage. It is quite a distance from the 25th row to the stage, especially when I have a few ushers to get by to get there. I decide to ask an usher if he'll let me go up there and of course, I am told "no". I return to my seat and meet the 11-year-old sitting next to me – it's his first show and he's super excited!!! Then I meet Julie's friend with the 2nd row seats and tell her that quite honestly, I would love to trade seats with her but she's not giving them up. I don't blame her; I probably would not have either. But, I had to ask. Sean tells me his plan to get a set list after the concert. I am excited!!! It is now just a few minutes to show time... I am anxious and excited.... and still trying to figure out how to get to the stage...

The lights go out, it is dark as night and the crowd starts to cheer. There is a spotlight and there is Elton ascending the steps to the stage! The noise is deafening! I am cheering and jumping and then I see it – the HUGE #60 displayed on the screen behind the stage and I hear the sweet notes of a familiar tune, "Sixty Years On". It is official – the concert had begun and, as always, the tears in my eyes are there. Elton plays a modified version of his 60th birthday concert. It is a great set for true fan... some songs you would only know if you owned the album or CD and of course, the classics. The live version of "Take Me to the Pilot", the foot-stomping, hand-clapping "Burn Down the Mission", the echoing sounds of "Rocketman".

I am on cloud nine, brought down a notch with the soulful "Sacrifice" and then my cloud crashed – Elton announced that his last album was his last, he introduced "The Bridge" and I cried through the whole thing. I just could not believe it. My sadness, however, only lasted a few more songs until he hit that one familiar note – the one note of the intro to "Bennie and the

Jets" and I am right back into dancing and cheering. Still in a little shock of the announcement but vowing to have a great time anyway! At this point, I know the show is going to end soon but I cannot see if people have left their seats to go to the stage. I need to have a plan to get to the stage and as soon as "Saturday..." was over, I made my move.

I don't get very far before the usher stops me and tells me that I can't get any closer – I am not even out of my section! So, I stay where she stopped me. After all, she is only doing her job and I don't want to get escorted out! I am jumping and waving my plate above my head trying to get Elton's attention (as if I am the only one trying to do this) and then I see her ... a fan leaving early ... coming toward me ... I have to act fast. "Are you leaving?" I ask her. She nods yes and I already have my hand out. All I say to her is "ticket!" to which she hands me her ticket stub and shouts "Row P, Row P".

Ok, I don't really care what row she is in; I am going to the stage! No one can stop me, because I have a ticket for that section! By this time, Elton is already halfway across the stage signing autographs. I am yelling at him as if he can hear me and people are noticing what I am trying to do and moving out of my way. Elton fans are great that way. I think I managed to get into the third row of seats before I decided to just climb over seats to get to the stage. I manage to do so only to look up and see the usher right in front of me.. uh-oh ... "Ma'am, you have to go back, you can't climb over seats".

UGGH!!! I abide because I am so close and cannot risk having to be escorted back to my seat. However, I am now in row 2 and Elton is almost done signing. I am not in the row in front of the piano. A fan lets me move down the row and I finally manage to get up to the stage but it is too late, he is done signing and seated at the piano and as much as I hope, I know he is not going to get up again just to come and sign my plate. However, I am now right up against the stage and I am not leaving. The best I can hope for is to at least get his attention. He is thanking the crowd and introducing "Your Song" which is his final song of the night. I am waving my plate above my head, shouting his name and then there it is... he makes eye contact with me, gives a little nod and that classic Elton smile. My mission is accomplished. Elton knew I was there. In that moment, the drive, the money spent and the exasperating trip from the 25th row to the stage is all worth it. Elton smiled at ME! I felt like the only person in that arena.

I savor the moment and then decide that I want to "say hi" to Davey and whoever else in the band I can get to see me. Davey sees me first, nods and smiles. Then Guy Babylon (keyboard) and Bob Birch (guitar) give me a little nod and a smile. I did not get the attention of Nigel or John Mahon but that's ok. Before I knew it, I heard the last words of "Your Song" and I know the show is over. Elton leaves to loud cheers but no one around me is leaving. It is almost as if time stood still for a moment, like no one can believe that Elton came, put on a fabulous show and left. Everyone else in the arena is leaving but those of us lucky to be that close to the stage like to linger a bit. I chatted with a few people who I recognized from previous shows but I can't remember their names. They recognized me and my plate though and I got a little taste of "being famous". It's kind of cool when another fan comes up and says, "Oh, it's you, did you get it signed tonight?" I feel sad to tell them no, but elated to tell them that he acknowledged me. We chat about how great the show was and look forward to seeing him again.

As Julie and I (Julie had been with me on my "journey" to the stage, cheering me on) go to leave the stage, I remember that I left my program under my seat. Sean had stayed at his seat until the end of the show but had left to go and get me the set list. Julie got back to our seats first and told me that the program was gone. I was disappointed for a moment but I am not upset about it. Some fan left the show that night with a "free" program. I left the show with the memory of a nod and a smile from Elton and an original set list. I think I got the better end of that deal! Another Elton adventure is over. I drove 14 hours and spent quite a bit of money to spend three hours with him. I am still a little tired and my voice a little scratchy but it is all worth it. I would do it all over again in a heartbeat. Until that next time, I have another great concert memory....

Life Lesson:

Persistence and perseverance are vital to success, but always, always follow the rules and honor your promises.

15
The Vision Becomes Reality

When God brought Valerie back into my life at that stoplight in 2001, we agreed to never lose touch with each other again. One of the many concerts we attended together was a trip halfway across the state of North Carolina to Winston-Salem for my thirteenth concert. This was one of the many concerts where we would drive to the concert city, attend the concert, and drive back home in a span of about twenty-four hours.

One of the most memorable trips together was to Charleston, South Carolina—my fifteenth time seeing Elton John in concert. We made a great traveling team; I would drive and Valerie would be on the phone, trying to get us closer seats. Having attended many more concerts than me up to this point, she knew the process of getting those coveted front-row seats—the same seats she was in when I met her back at the Roanoke concert. The following is the email summary I sent to family and friends after the concert.

Elton John and The Band
North Charleston, SC
North Charleston Coliseum
Friday, November 9, 2007
On Friday, my friend Valerie and I were off on another adventure to see Elton John in concert. The destination this time was North Charleston, SC. However, this concert was different. It was the first time that Valerie and I would attend the show together and

sit together to enjoy our favorite musician.

We arrived to pick up tickets and decided to go to the parking lot behind the venue to see the tour buses that were lined up there. As luck would have it, there was a very nice security guard at the entrance to the gate who informed us that Elton would be arriving at "any moment". He then told us that we were welcome to stand on the sidewalk and wait there. He would get the call on the radio when Elton was arriving.

Valerie and I heard the sirens "announcing" Elton's arrival. He does, after all, get a police escort. He must have been in a huge hurry because I only got a brief glimpse of him sitting in the back of the SUV. What an exciting moment! I had watched Elton arrive! Now we had to race to our hotel to check in and get dressed for the show.

My evening got better when we arrived back at the venue. By virtue of attending so many shows, Valerie knows many people who work closely with Elton and his band. She pointed out Elton's piano tech. She then introduced me to Davey Johnstone's guitar tech. Valerie had gifts for him and Davey that she successfully delivered. I then met some fellow fans Valerie knows from previous shows, including Carol - her best friend from Charlotte. That is always a great thrill, to meet other Elton fanatics! Many had driven or flown in from up north for this one. (After the show, we hung out with Carole at the hotel and she had some great Elton stories to share. I also met her 98 1/2 year-old mom and her husband, Joe, who is a great fan as well. Poor Joe missed his first EJ show to care for Carole's mom at the hotel.)

At a few minutes to 8pm we took our seats and waited for Elton to arrive on stage. The venue was sold out, and as soon as the lights went out, the crowd started clapping and cheering! It was a fabulous crowd and very excited to see Elton. We hear the first sounds of "Funeral for a Friend" and Elton appears onstage to an *eruption of cheers. The concert has begun! I am in a moment that I can't believe is actually happening.*

This concert is so special. You see, my seat next to Valerie for this show was none other than front row center stage. Yes, FRONT ROW, CENTER STAGE. Throughout the show, I was able to easily get the attention of the band members and have them acknowledge me in some way. I was able to see the stage camera guy set up his shot and take some video of my license plate that then was put up on the big screen for all the fans to see. Since I knew it was happening, it was cool to look up on the screen and see my plate being "shown off". Valerie succeeded in her goal to once again receive the first guitar pick of the night from Davey. Life is good.

It was the best experience after they performed "Candle in the Wind" to not have to fight my way up to the stage or worry about getting stopped by an usher. I had to go about five feet to get right up to the stage. I was able to get to "my spot" (the spot I had chosen before the show began) right up at the stage, directly in front of Elton without having to fight for it or worry that I wasn't going to get there. I sang to Elton and he sang to me. His purple sunglasses were light enough so that I could see right into his eyes and know that when he looked at me and smiled, he was looking directly at me.

I could see my reflection in the black gloss of the piano leg. I was able to prop my "RCKTMNFN" license plate up on the stage so he could see it. When he came to the stage to sign autographs, I anxiously awaited my turn and was thrilled when he took my plate and signed it. (It has now been autographed three times by Elton). A few moments later, Elton came my way again, and I stuck my hand up in the air to try to get a handshake. I got a "finger tip" instead but that's better than nothing. Once he sat back at the piano, he played "Don't Let the Sun Go Down on Me" and I started to get a little sad. I knew there was only one more song to go and then my evening with Elton would be over. Before the final song, Elton thanked everyone for coming and for our support of him. He dedicated "Your Song" to "each and every one of you". Too soon it seemed, the song was over and Elton was up from the piano bench, waving good-bye to the crowd. The show was over but my memories will remain forever. I am living proof that dreams come true. My very first Elton John show was sixteen years ago. I remember thinking the first time I heard him sing "I think it's going to be a long, long time" from "Rocket Man" that it would indeed be a "long, long time" before I would have an opportunity like I had Friday night. It has been a long, long time – sixteen years!. Through all the years and all the concerts I stayed focused on my dream and took advantage of opportunities and situations as they occurred. You may remember that I met Valerie at an Elton show in Roanoke, VA on February 19, 1999. Our love of Elton made us great acquaintances and over the past few years we have become friends. She is the reason I had a front row seat.

This concert memory will be so very special to me for a long, long time… take a front row seat on your concert of life and your dreams will come true too ;)

Nothing is as real as a dream. The world can change around you, but your dream will not. Responsibilities need not erase it. Duties need not obscure it.

> *"Because the dream is within you, no one can take it away."*
> *Tom Clancy*

Side note: Do you remember the story of my first concert when I envisioned myself sitting in the front row, center stage? That vision came true at this concert. I know now that creating the image in your mind of where you want to be is a very powerful tool to making goals achievable.

Life Lesson:

Decide what you want and envision yourself experiencing it. Getting that picture in your mind and remembering it is an important part of the goal-achieving process.

16
<u>Cramming</u>

It may seem ridiculous to some people that I will fly out of state to attend an Elton John concert. These days, it's more out of convenience and necessity, since the wear and tear of travel, the adrenaline rush and crash of attending multiple concerts at one time, and the years that have passed since my first concert at age nineteen have made it more difficult to make the drive home.

For my sixteenth concert, however, the flight was more a matter of convenience. Valerie and I flew from North Carolina to New York City, had a few adventures including the concert, and flew home the next day. I don't think it's possible that we could have crammed any more activities into the little time we were in New York. It was quite the adventure. This is the email summary I sent out to friends and family after the trip. (added in its original form)

Elton John Solo Show
April 9, 2008
Radio City Music Hall
One morning, I answered the phone to hear, "Elton John will be doing a concert in NYC and I am debating whether or not to go – by the way, tickets go on sale in about 5 minutes." So, a quick decision was made – we were going – and it was a whirlwind few hours to buy the tickets, secure a hotel room and book our airline tickets.
I was excited to be seeing Elton again although not too happy

with the knowledge that there would be no front row seat at this concert. This show was to be an experience for me as it was a fundraiser for Hillary Clinton's Presidential campaign and I do not support her. I knew that in buying the ticket, I would be contributing to her campaign but I was going for Elton and I was going with Valerie. Our last trip together was so much fun and I knew I was in for more of the same.

The experience started Tuesday night with a phone call from Valerie that she had gotten us tickets to a special interview Wednesday afternoon. The taping would begin at 3pm, we had to be there at 1:30pm and our plane landed at LGA at noon. WOW! The interview was one of a series for a show produced by Elton John. Elvis Costello would be interviewing famous people about the impact of music in their lives. (Sadly, we missed Elton John's interview on Tuesday). Former President Bill Clinton was to be the guest on Wednesday afternoon.

Once we landed at LGA, we took a car to the hotel (we stayed at the Crowne Plaza at Times Square). This was quite an experience as well! A quick trip to check into the hotel, leaving our bags with the concierge and we were off in a dash to grab lunch and wait in line for the interview taping. We opted to eat at Lenny's near the NBC studios - this certainly was not our neighborhood sandwich shop! It was the typical bustling of a New York eatery and I had to be a quick student of "the system" to order, pay for and pick up the food. I ended up ordering the first thing on the menu that, after reading all the ingredients in the sandwich, I thought, "I'll eat all of that!" There wasn't time to peruse the menu in that place!

We ate lunch while waiting in line to attend the interview and chatted with some interesting people including one lady who had attended Elton's interview the day prior. It was then off to the security check and up the elevators to the Studio where

Saturday Night Live is performed. (This would be more exciting for me if I actually watched SNL, but I don't). We were taken to our seats and I was excited that we were in the third row from the stage! It was exciting to be part of something that will be aired on TV! Elvis Costello played a few musical numbers and then it was time for the main event! Again, while I do not support the Clinton's, it was a real experience for me to be about 20 feet away from President Clinton. Additionally, it was interesting to listen to him speak about something other than politics for a while although there were a few comments here and there. I learned that he is a great student of music, especially of jazz, which influenced him to play the saxophone. I was also interested to learn that he had more music scholarships to attend college than academic scholarships.

When the interview was over, he did shake hands with a few people but not ours. Two musicians, unknown to me, closed out the taping and it was off to our next decision – do we go back to the hotel or do we go hang out at Radio City Music Hall and try to see Elton arrive. Yeah, for us, that wasn't a hard decision to make.

After what seemed like forever, he was there – about five feet away from us. I said "Hi" to him but he was walking with his head down and was in a hurry to get in the building. As an added bonus for me, I got to see Elton's two Cocker Spaniels, Arthur and Marilyn, arrive as well. They are cute!

Shortly afterward, we were asked by NYPD to move down the block a bit and we knew that Hillary must be on her way. When she arrived, she stopped and waved at the crowd. There was a nice size crowd and it was exciting to be in the midst of all the excitement and energy people have for her and her campaign. We were also able to see President Bill Clinton arrive along with Chelsea. It was really neat to see them in person, rather than just on a TV screen. Then, it was off to wait in line to get into RCMH. It was a slow-moving line as security was very tight. We walked through a metal detector, were wanded and had our bags searched. Our dinner that evening consisted of hotdogs from the concession stand and then it was off to our seats. The funny story about our seats was that Valerie started in her original seat, I sat next to her (not in my assigned seat), we moved down to the front row (of the mezzanine), those people showed up so we ended up moving to a different front row and luckily, stayed there the entire night!

The 8pm concert did not start until after 9pm (remember the long security process?) and, again, it was quite an experience and I probably would have enjoyed it much more if I supported Hillary. Her campaign manager spoke, then President Bill Clinton spoke and lastly, Hillary spoke. The energy in that building was unreal and very exciting to witness. The people there just exploded in applause when Hillary was introduced.

Finally, the moment I had come for arrived and Elton was introduced to the crowd. He played an almost two hour set list including my favorite, "Rocketman". What a show to see – just Elton and the piano. We could feel the music vibrating in our seats – I LOVE live concerts!

Fortunately, there were large TV screens that showed the concert because from where we were sitting, all we could see was tiny Elton not the "I have front row seats Elton." All too soon, the show was over but the next phase of our exciting day/evening was just beginning. (keep in mind that we were doing so well to stay awake as Valerie had not slept the night before and I had been up since 6am). After I swore to Valerie to keep it a secret, we went to the hotel where she thought Elton was staying to attempt to get an autograph upon his return from the concert. Within the two hours that we "hung out" at the hotel, we saw his partner David leave the hotel and Elton's manager arrive at the hotel but there was no sign of Elton. We had just decided to leave the area when Valerie said, "Hey, that guy across the street looks like Rick". (I had met him at the Charleston show). When I looked up, I immediately thought the same thing and we both shouted to him. As it turns out, it WAS him – what a coincidence! We chatted for a while and ultimately concluded that Elton was not coming back to the hotel. It was then (by now it is about 2am) that we decided to go to the Waldorf – Astoria hotel (I had never been there) as it was the site of a fundraiser that Elton attended Tuesday night. What an amazing place! At 2am, it is not bustling with activity which gave us opportunity to see the grand ballroom and tour around a bit. A short taxi ride to back to our hotel ultimately ended the adventure of the day and I was asleep by 3 am.

What a whirlwind of adventure and a great experience! Within a span of almost twelve hours, I sat in the same room with a former President and witnessed his interview, attended an event for a woman running for President, saw Elton John play a solo set, saw David Furnish and Elton's manager and stood in the Grand Ballroom of the Waldorf-Astoria hotel. Never mind the money I spent on the ticket, the travel and the lodging, the experience was once-in-a-lifetime and certainly priceless.

Life Lessons:

Time is a limited resource. Make the most of the time you are given.

17
Crowd Control

My fourteenth Elton John concert took place in Charlotte, North Carolina, in March 2007. My seat was on the floor, but several rows back from the stage on Elton's side. It doesn't matter how many concerts I go to, I still have the same level of excitement as I did with the very first one. Maybe I don't cry anymore when the opening notes begin, but I sure do get misty-eyed. I love everything about the concert experience and I show it; I sing and dance and always have a great time. I've developed the consistent habit of bringing my license plate (an old one, not the current one on my car) to the concerts. If I get up to the stage for an autograph, that's what I hand to Elton for his signature.

During this particular concert, I often held my plate above my head, trying to see if I could get Elton's attention from my seat in the tenth row. I had no idea if he could see it, but I did notice that several people around me saw it every time I held it up. When the time came for fans to approach the edge of the stage, I decided to take a chance and see if I could get past the usher. I wasn't a few steps from my row when the usher blocked my path. I pleaded my case.

"See here, where Elton has autographed it before? I just want to run up to the stage, grab an autograph, and I'll be right back," I said. The usher shook her head and shifted position so I could not get past her. I started to ask again, and heard the crowd around me chanting,

"Let her go! Let her go!" The crowd around me, the same

crowd that had seen me holding my plate up during the concert was helping me plead me case!

I looked at the usher and asked, "Please? I promise I will come straight back here!" She hesitated for a moment and, as the chants grew louder, nodded in agreement with the crowd. I took off for the stage and arrived with just enough time to get my plate to Elton from the edge of the stage. Remaining true to my word, I returned to my seat, holding the plate up high, and pointing to the space where he signed it.

As I approached my row, the same crowd who pleaded with me began to clap and cheer. Several people around me congratulated me, and as I looked back to the usher to tell her thank you, she just looked at me and smiled. I will never forget her kindness in that moment.

Life Lessons:

1. *When you see someone attempting to achieve a goal, cheer them on!*
2. *When you have the chance, be kind. Acts of kindness are never forgotten.*

18
Problem Solving, Part 2

One issue with problem solving is that if it's not the right solution, it doesn't work. This turned out to be true with my "making more money" solution after I decided I needed a better financial management plan. I did make more money, but I didn't manage it well. I now know making more money doesn't solve financial problems. In order to manage money better, I needed a complete mindset shift. I had to delete all the old habits I had with money and create new habits in their place. I needed to think differently about the concept of money, and I needed a new plan.

This realization came in December 2009 when I hit financial rock bottom. The boys were five and four at the time and, in hindsight, I had gotten sucked into the commercialization of Christmas. I wanted that Norman Rockwell-type of Christmas morning, where the boys awoke and rushed down the hallway to see what Santa had brought them—certainly everything on their Christmas lists and more. We were still living paycheck-to-paycheck at the time, and I hadn't planned and saved for Christmas. I was still in the mindset of flipping the calendar over to December and then frantically getting everything set up for the perfect Christmas Day celebration. At this point, I was certainly more concerned with the commercialization of Christmas than I was about the true meaning. The boys were more excited about Santa coming than they were about celebrating the birth of Jesus.

In the early part of December, I was sitting at the computer, perusing the online store of a big-name shopping site and adding items to my cart. I had three or four credit cards before me and knew how much I could add to each one. At this time, we were almost maxed out on all of our cards, and so I had to put a little on one, a little on another, and a little on another. It never occurred to me to pick one card and set a limit for shopping. I needed to make sure the boys' first Christmas understanding Santa was a memorable one for them.

I don't profess to hear a directive straight from God very often, but when I do, it is clear to me. Often, I need Him to get the message to me at least three times before I act on something, but in this case, it was very clear. To this day, I have a hard time explaining it, because it seems weird that it would happen to me. As I sat at the computer adding purchases to my cart, this clear thought came to mind: "You are doing this wrong."

"What am I doing wrong?" I wondered. "I've done online shopping before, I know what I'm doing."

Then I realized what I was doing. I was going against everything I had been taught about the real meaning of Christmas. I had allowed material things to become more important than spiritual things. I was creating a negative financial situation for my family by putting Christmas on credit and adding to our debt. I immediately felt guilty. I didn't know what I should do. I couldn't cancel Christmas because we didn't have the money. No way was I going to go against the societal teachings of Christmas as a commercial holiday. Who does that? Certainly, not me, and certainly not this year; the year the boys were so eagerly awaiting the arrival of Santa on Christmas morning.

So, I did the next best thing. I bargained with God and made Him a deal: the typical "if this, then that" solution. I decided I was going to go through with my plan, but I promised God I would find a better way for me to manage my money, and I would not be in this same situation the following year. Did I know what that solution was? No, but God did. God already had a plan. At the time, I failed to recognize it; I chose to ignore it. Now I know this was not my first call to action from Him but, in fact, my third.

As a former teacher, I decided I needed to create a lesson plan for personal finance and, once created, I would follow that plan. I took the week between Christmas and New Year's to research and develop the idea that I would start my plan on January 1, 2010. At the time, David Bach, Suze Orman, and that *Mad Money* guy, Jim Cramer, were all over television. I went to their websites, I read their books, and I subscribed to their email lists. I took the information that I liked from each person and started writing out a plan.

In the midst of this planning, I thought of my friend Katrina who, a few months earlier, had told me about a new money management course she was taking at her church called Financial Peace University by Dave Ramsey. At the time, I wasn't willing to accept the fact that we had a problem managing money. After all, almost everyone I knew had the same financial issues that we had, so I thought it was normal. Katrina, however, was so excited about getting out of debt and writing a budget and she told me so every time I saw her. She and I were in the same social circles, and I knew that once I started this new plan, I would also start telling others about it. That's just the way I am—a walking, vocal advertisement for all the things I love. I decided I needed to add in some of that "Dave Ramsey stuff" so I could tell Katrina I was doing some of it as part of my plan.

With great hesitation, I entered the web address and clicked *Enter*. When the home screen appeared on my laptop, I scanned the text and a feeling came over me. I knew *this* was the plan I needed. I'd love to say I heard angels singing and trumpets blaring and a bright light like the sun illuminated from my laptop screen, but none of that happened. The more I read, the more I just knew this was the solution I'd been seeking. I connected with Dave Ramsey's story of going bankrupt (although we were not at that point), and I loved that his plan was biblically-based and a step-by-step process.

I knew in my soul this was the plan I should follow. I understood the plan that God had so patiently tried to show me over the last few months. Little did I know the impact that acting on this knowledge would have for our future.

Life Lesson:

When you hit rock bottom, the only way to go is up. Find someone who has been where you are (or worse) and found their way out. Follow the plan that worked for them.

19
<u>The Solution</u>

On December 31, 2009, I took $99 off the top of that week's paycheck and purchased the Financial Peace University at-home study course. I discarded all the other plans I had made from other financial gurus and decided to follow only this plan. I wanted this thing called *financial peace*.

My husband wasn't happy with the idea. We both knew we didn't have $99 to spend on a course to teach us about money. Our brains told us this money management stuff wasn't rocket science. But I knew I needed something totally different than what I was doing. I needed to make an investment in our family's financial future and make drastic changes.

Despite his disagreement, I argued that we needed this to become better with our money and I felt like this time, this plan could really work. I managed the checkbook, so I took it upon myself to make that purchase. I was scared. We were living paycheck-to-paycheck at the time. I didn't know how would I manage the month of January $99 short, but I had faith that this was God's plan for us, and I took the leap. It wasn't the first time I had taken a leap; I entered the commitment of marriage after meeting Jack online and only knowing him for eighteen months. At this point, we had been married nine years and had two children, so that leap worked out great! I had no doubt this leap would yield the same result. It had to; we had no other choice.

I opted for the online course so I could get started right away. I figured I could go on to the following lesson as soon as I finished the first, and completing this program became my life's purpose. I was a diligent student of all things Dave Ramsey and followed the process exactly as it was laid out. It wasn't until I started the program that I fully realized the mess we were in. I knew we were living paycheck-to-paycheck and had no emergency fund. I knew we had no plan for our financial future. I knew we had debt. What I didn't know was how much.

When I worked with the direct sales company, there was some event where I added something wrong and we made a big joke out of it. I said, "That's why I'm not the math teacher!" It's not that I'm bad at math, but at the time, I was not as interested in numbers and their functions. To me, math was predictable and boring. Words were much more fun.

I preface this story with that idea in mind. When I completed our debt snowball sheet, part of the process was to add up all the debt. We had six credit cards, two vehicle loans, my student loan, the mortgage, and the home equity line of credit (HELOC). The "consumer debt" part of that—the part I focused on paying off per the baby steps—was everything except the mortgage and the HELOC. The first time I added the total, I knew I had made a mistake. The second time I added the numbers, I got the same answer, but still thought it was a mistake. Several more times of adding later, and I was dumbfounded. I could not believe the number staring back at me from my paper: $43,544.00.

That number was more than half of our income. That number was hard to accept and hard to grasp. I knew we had debt, but I had no idea the amount was that high. How in the world were we supposed to pay all of that off? Remember, I was a stay-at-home mom at the time. All I knew was that there was hope. Hope was there because Dave Ramsey had gone bankrupt and pulled himself up out of that mess. We were not bankrupt. We hadn't lost everything. There was still hope.

Day after day, I studied the process of budgeting. Over time and through much trial and error, I created a budget that fit our family. The hardest part of the process was giving up credit cards. It's still amazing to me how emotionally attached I'd become to them, as if they were my own little financial security blankets. With the budget and the debt snowball in place, I made the plan work. I made sure I got a return on my investment. I had no other choice. I had promised God we would not be in the same financial situation for Christmas of 2010. There were some things, however, I wasn't willing to give up in order to become debt-free. I still had a dream to pursue and, despite the plan, I wasn't willing to put my dream on hold as a consequence for bad financial decisions.

Life Lesson:
*There are often many solutions to a problem. The one that will work is the one that is right for **you**.*

20
<u>Opportunity Knocks</u>

There were quite a few things I was willing to give up while we were working on becoming debt-free. We had to either decrease spending or increase income to meet our financial goals. We ended up doing both. In creating a budget, we drastically reduced our spending. One area in which we did this was our grocery budget. We gave up wants and purchased needs. That's not to say that we didn't ever purchase something we wanted, but it wasn't a weekly occurrence like it was before. We watched our water and electrical usage to lower our bills and figured out how to be more efficient with car trips to maximize our gas budget. The boys were five and four at the time, and involved in a few extracurricular activities. We pulled them out of those, too. They were upset at first, but because they were young, they got over it faster. Over time, we figured out how to create and follow a budget that worked for our family.

The one thing I wasn't willing to give up, however, was seeing Elton John in concert. I did have to give up putting concert trips on a credit card, because that's part of the deal: no more credit cards. You can't dig out of a hole if you are still digging, so I made that commitment.

That was one of the hardest things about becoming debt-free. I had used credit cards since I was eighteen years old. When I got close to my limit, the credit card company was so kind to increase my limit. It was such a normal part of my everyday life, and I had made the voluntary decision to break that habit. If I wasn't willing to give up seeing Elton in concert and I voluntary gave up using credit cards, I had no other option than to save cash to go.

Often, this meant I did not know until about a week before the concert whether I was going or not. Every time Valerie would call me about going to a concert I would say, "I don't know if I can go. I don't have enough money yet." I had developed a strong sense of doing what it takes to earn the money to go, because the regret of not being able to go to the sixtieth birthday concert was always there. I did not want to experience that again, especially when the concert venues were within driving distance of our home. I could not tolerate again the ridicule I received because I was a big fan and I didn't go. Oh, yes, even well into adulthood, I am still being made fun of because I am pursuing this dream of meeting Elton John. Not going to the concert only gave the doubters and the naysayers more fuel for the fire, and I hated that.

We started our debt-free journey on January 1, 2010. At that time, we were living-paycheck-to-paycheck. We had no money in savings and no plan for our financial future. We had over $43,000 of consumer debt apart from our mortgage. Strictly following the plan meant that I should have used the money I would have spent seeing Elton John toward paying down the debt. I wasn't willing to do that. Pursuing my dream was more important than paying off my debt. However, my number one reason for becoming debt-free was to have money to pursue my dream. I know it doesn't make sense, but I had to figure out a way to pursue my dream while still paying off debt.

Jack and I spent a lot of time discussing if I would get a job working outside the home. Ultimately, we decided it didn't make sense. He does not work a normal nine-to-five job, and even though the boys were in school during the day, I would have to find someone to watch them while we were both at work. Sometimes, that would mean I'd have to pay a sitter. It didn't make financial sense to work a minimum-wage job, only to have to pay a sitter or daycare. My "job," therefore, became learning how to become better with money. I became a student of personal finance, reading books and blogs, listening to *The Dave Ramsey Show*, and constantly tweaking the budget to use it to our advantage.

I made lists, graphs, and charts to mark our progress. I watched *Extreme Couponing* on TLC to learn how to save more money on our groceries. I clipped, sorted, and organized coupons, then went to the store to put into practice what I had learned from the show. Sometimes I would save big; sometimes I wouldn't. When I didn't, I went back to learning and figuring out what I did wrong. Yes, I created a stockpile, and yes, I got things for free. Super Double coupon events were my favorite weeks of the year. I could fine-tune our grocery budget to the point in which I came under budget and created savings. Most of the time, that savings went toward paying off debt, but when it was Elton season, that money went toward concert trips.

As you might imagine, a concert trip is not cheap. Traveling means extra gas money, hotel money, food money, and of course, concert ticket money. I wasn't sitting in the cheap seats, either. On average, I would spend $100 on a concert ticket. Why? Because I had become a seat snob. Once I experienced sitting on the first few rows, I did not want to sit anywhere else. After all, Elton won't know I'm there if he can't see me, right?

As soon as I decided which concerts I was attending, I set up a plan to save money to go. Between January 1, 2010, and September 27, 2013, I attended five Elton John concerts. Each time, I had just enough money to go, and that money always showed up about a week before the trip. I cash-flowed every single one.

How did that happen? God had a plan.

I needed a way to earn extra money without compromising the boys' schedules, so I would have to pay for daycare. I quit my direct sales company job in 2009 when the stock market crashed. My business crashed, too, because I was selling things that people wanted, not needed. I didn't want to push through the struggle of running a business and feeling like I was begging people to host parties and buy products, so I quit. To find a job with a flexible schedule, I thought about going back into direct sales and found a company I thought would work. It didn't.

I guess I was just burned out by the whole direct sales model, even though I think it's a great opportunity for some people. I know many people who make their living with direct sales companies and they love it. It's just not for me. My answer to a job with a flexible schedule that provided good income came in the form of a phone call.

"Hi, Melissa, this is Donna."

"Hi, Donna, what's up?"

"I have a client whose dog sitter canceled on her at the last minute. I think she lives close to you and she is in desperate need of someone to watch her dogs this weekend. You have four dogs; do you dog sit?"

Without hesitation, I replied, "Yes! Yes, I do!"

"Great," she said. "How much do you charge?"

Yes, I owned four dogs, and yes, I've had dogs almost my entire life. I was perfectly capable of taking care of someone else's dogs. The problem was that I didn't have a business at that point. I'd had a business when I was in high school and dog sat in my neighborhood, but that wasn't a real business. I was just a high school kid who wanted to spend more time with more dogs, so I got paid to watch other people's dogs. I never saved or invested any of that money. I didn't have a business model. But

I did have experience, which is why I told Donna that I did dog sit. Most entrepreneurs will tell you that one way they got started was by saying yes to an opportunity and then figuring out a way to make it happen.

"Well, that depends on how many dogs they have, where they live, and how long they want me to watch them. Why don't you have your client call me and I'll discuss my fee with her?"

Donna replied, "Okay, great. She'll call you soon."

I wasn't exactly sure what soon meant, but I knew I had to act fast. I quickly googled local boarding kennels to find out their rates. The prices were about the same and the services offered were as well. I wasn't thinking about competitive rates or growth and scale of a business at this point; I knew I needed a dollar amount to give her when she called. I decided that my rate would be $30 a day and would include checking on the house, getting the mail, and watering plants.

When Kathi called, we discussed this and she asked me several questions to get to know me better. Donna was the groomer for our dog, Ooch. Kathi knew Donna because she groomed her two West Highland White Terriers, Schnucke and Shotzi. When Kathi's dog sitter canceled last-minute, she called Donna for help. Donna thought of me, and that's how I got connected with Kathi. During our phone call, we decided on a time for me to go over and meet the dogs.

Not only was Kathi's house within a bike ride's distance from our house, but her dogs were so sweet. We went over their daily routine and feeding schedule, Kathi gave me a key to her house, and I got my first dog sitting job.

My dog sitting money was not budgeted. Although I became the regular sitter for Schnucke and Shotzi, it was irregular income. I only got paid when Kathi went out of town. She was so pleased with the job I did, she asked me if I would do it for other people. Of course, I said I would.

I decided, though, that I would only dog sit for people in my town. At some point, I decided to post on Facebook that I was dog sitting, and was hired by friends. Over time, my business grew through referrals, and I continue that business to this day. All my clients have come directly through referrals. I do not do any outside advertising or marketing except for the occasional post on Facebook. I have several regular clients and, in fact, have been given my own key to their homes. My regular clients just contact me with the dates they need me, I'll tell them the total fee, and they leave cash or a check for me. It's a wonderful arrangement. The business has evolved to more than just dog sitting, too. I have looked after homes with no pets during extended vacations. I have taken care of ducks, chickens, and cats. I even have one client with two dogs, a cat, and a bearded dragon!

This business solved the problem of needing money to go see Elton. Each time I needed concert money, someone would need me to watch their house or their pets. It just happened that way. I always had enough money to go without compromising our plan to become debt-free.

Life Lesson:
Say yes to opportunity. Figure out how to make it happen.

21
<u>Purpose</u>

Valerie and I attended five concerts together while I was digging out of debt. There were many things I was willing to compromise to save money and pay down debt, but foregoing attending concerts was not one of them. However, without a credit card to fund my adventures, the decision to go was not often made until the last minute. I could only go if I saved the cash and had enough for the entire trip.

It was during this time I learned I could eat for little and go to grocery stores instead of restaurants when I traveled. Valerie and I drove separately, but stayed at hotels with free breakfast. I was learning what it meant to be frugal. I found that, if I had a cooler, I could pack sandwiches and drinks from home for the trip. I learned I didn't need to buy something from the merchandise vendors at every concert; no, that money was better spent on the tickets.

At this point, it had become normal for me to sit in the first three rows after the experience of sitting in the front row. That experience is worth so much more than anything I could buy from a vendor. I was learning that if I gave my money a purpose, it would fulfill that purpose. It's not easy to make decisions based on money because we are taught to have it all whenever we want it.

My first cash-flow concert was in Asheville, North Carolina, in 2010, almost a year into our getting-out-of-debt plan. The next three were the first "batch" concerts I attended—Roanoke,

Virginia, to Raleigh, North Carolina, to Richmond, Virginia—three nights in a row in three different cities. The last was in Winston-Salem in April 2013. The unique thing about each of these concerts is that I often didn't know if I could go or not until the last possible minute. It was during this time I learned there was always going to be a ticket for me to attend if I was willing to pay the price, whether it be time or money, for the seat I wanted.

Life Lesson:
Money serves a purpose. It's our job to tell it where to go.

22
People Are People

Asheville, NC
November 2010
Concert 18

It's a seven-hour drive from my hometown to Asheville, North Carolina. That's one way. However, it was worth the trip to see Elton John and Leon Russell perform as part of The Union tour. Valerie accompanied me on this trip and we passed the time in the car with some great conversation. And yes, while we don't normally travel on concert day, the plan was to drive seven hours there, attend the concert, and then drive seven hours home the next day.

Elton John and the band had recently performed a concert that was streamed either online or on TV from The Beacon Theater in New York. While watching it, I learned about the background singers. These four ladies were invited to perform with Elton on the album and on tour. I missed the introductions and didn't know who they were by name.

In Asheville, while standing in the hotel lobby with Valerie, I saw a woman walking toward the elevators near us. She was very nicely dressed, like she was going to an event. I suddenly realized I recognized her from The Beacon Theater concert. She was one of the background singers. I nudged Valerie and asked, "Hey, isn't that lady one of the background singers? She is, right?" Before Valerie could answer me directly, I heard her say, "Oh! It's Ms. Tata Vega."

Oh, yes, it's Tata Vega. I had no idea who Tata Vega was, but I bet since I recognized her, and Valerie knew her name, that she was, indeed, one of the background singers. She paused in stride and we introduced ourselves. We chatted for at least thirty minutes. She was astounded and humbled that we drove seven hours just to attend the concert. I thought to myself, *You are a backup singer for Sir Elton John and I'm standing here talking to you like normal conversation!*

She repeatedly told us how blessed she was and how God had such a big part in her life. She was so genuine, down-to-earth, and humble. Such an amazing encounter. Once we arrived at the venue, we had the opportunity to meet the three other ladies who sang with Tata: Rose Stone, Lisa Stone, and Jean Witherspoon. I asked for and received an autograph from each one on the printed picture of my RKTMNFN2 license plate.

I didn't recognize their names until someone mentioned to me that Rose Stone was from Sly and the Family Stone, a popular soul/R&B band from the late '60s through early '80s. I'm not too familiar with that genre of music, but I did recognize the name of the band.

When I got home, I did some research on Tata Vega. She is well-known in the gospel community and has had several jobs as a backup singer for many well-known musical artists. She is also a recording artist. I could not believe a woman of her significance was so down-to-earth in meeting us. Because of that meeting, I began following her on social media. It was through this that I found out about the movie Twenty Feet from Stardom. The movie is a historical account of people who make their living as background singers. It a fascinating look into the world of music and being a support to the main act, but having just as important a role in pulling off the concert experience. My favorite line from that movie was from Ms. Tata herself:

"It's more than leaning on your talent. You gotta be disciplined. You gotta get up in the morning. Opportunity's knocking. Open the door, kiddo."

I did the same with the other ladies and was amazed at what I found. I never would have known they were such a big deal in the music industry. They were all so humble and down-to-earth. This would not be my first encounter with a member of Elton's band this trip.

Later that night, while eating at a restaurant, Valerie became giddy when she spotted two guys she recognized sitting at a nearby table. She walked over to them, I followed, and the gentlemen invited is to sit with them.

When the men introduced themselves, I finally put their faces to names. One of them was Elton John's piano technician, and the other was Davey Johnstone's guitar technician. To say I was star struck is an understatement. I mean, these two are the guys responsible for *Elton's* piano and *Davey's* guitar. Elton's piano tech makes sure it is tuned and taken care of to Elton's satisfaction. He participates in the sound check at every concert. He plays the same exact keys that Elton John plays, on the same exact piano that Elton John plays. The same with Davey's guitar tech; he makes sure the guitars are tuned, cleaned, and polished. He is the one who walks out on the stage in between songs and helps Davey switch out guitars. He is the one who helps Davey replace a guitar strap or makes sure he has enough picks and everything else involved in the care of the guitars. For purposes of their privacy, I'll call these guys *piano guy* and *guitar guy*.

So, there I am, sitting at the table with Valerie, piano guy, and guitar guy. She has obviously maintained some sort of cordial relationship with them, because they are chatting away like old friends catching up over dinner. I just sat there, completely in awe to be where I was. At the risk of opening my mouth and saying something stupid, I sat quietly, which is very uncharacteristic of me.

At some point, someone asked me to join in on the conversation, and I think I must have said something articulate like, "You guys have the best job in the world! I mean, you are the piano tech for Elton John and you are the guitar tech for Davey Johnstone. You travel all over the world with Elton John and the band and you—you are the piano tech and the guitar tech!"

Keep in mind that I cannot play either instrument, so it's not like I had any aspiration of doing their jobs, but I was blown away by these guys' careers. In the absence of something else to say, I just kept repeating myself. I couldn't think about anything else.

Guitar guy then asked me, "Well, what do you do?"

Ugh. In my mind, I thought I had the least glamorous, most uninteresting job in the entire world. However, I needed to answer honestly, without making anything up to impress him. He seemed like a nice enough guy to have a conversation with, so I answered, "Oh, I'm just a stay-at-home mom."

"A stay-at-home mom?" he exclaimed, "*That* is awesome!"
What did he just say?

Before I could respond, he proceeded, "That is the most awesome job in the whole world! How cool is it that you get to stay home with your kids and do mom stuff and not have to work outside the home? You must have some great adventures, and I think your job is the best! You know why?"

I must have stared blankly at him, so he continued, "I can never be a stay-at-home mom. I am thankful to have the job I have, but it is my job. Anyone else can do this job. This is a great job in this industry, but if I leave, someone else will be around to take my place. I love my job, but I could never, ever do your job, and that's why I think your job is awesome!"

Piano guy nodded in agreement. They both reiterate that they love their jobs, even though sometimes it's hard to travel and be away from family. And that most of the time, they don't get to do tourist things in the cities they visit because they are working. For them, traveling is work. It's long hours on flights and buses. It's making sure everything is done to perfection every night and that the instruments, which cost hundreds of thousands of dollars, are well cared-for and ready to go for every concert.

I could see what was happening. They were giving back to me what I have given to them—that sense of awe and wonder over what they do for a living. And you know what, it made sense to me. We are all just people. We are all just doing what we love. Piano guy and guitar guy have a job doing what they love to do. I have a job as a mom—not "just" a stay-at-home mom.

That one conversation changed my perspective about what I do. It also helped me realize that these guys are regular people, too. They have families and bills to pay and jobs to do, just like you and I do. They wake up every day and go to work. My job is important, too, not just something to be ho-hum about because I happen to not think it's very exciting or adventurous.

I never grew up with dream of being a stay-at-home mom. I always felt like there had to be something more than just spending the days with two boys, who at this point were five and four. I'm not "crafty" mom or "host a playdate" mom or "hang out at the park all day" mom.

I was a better mom because they were in school during the day, but one was in full-day kindergarten and one was in half-day preschool. I felt there had to be something more, but my time was so broken up during the day I didn't have it to do anything else except be "just a mom." When I told other people I was a stay-at-home mom, I generally got the response of, "Oh, must be nice," or, "You are so lucky; I wish I could do that," or, "What *do* you do all day?"

Since I wasn't the crafty mom, or the classroom mom, or the PTA mom, I guess there was a perception that being a stay-at-home mom wasn't enough. That, of course, translated into my perception that I wasn't enough. I didn't think it was nice or that I was lucky. I didn't know what I did all day, because there was no structure to my day other than what time I had to take the boys to and from school. My day was spent doing mom things like cleaning and grocery shopping and planning. I bounced from one thing to the next, never finishing one task, so it felt like I got nothing accomplished.

Coming from a career as a high school teacher and transitioning to the life of a stay-at-home mom wasn't going very well for me and by this time, I had been home with the boys for almost five years.

Now I understand being the mom of two boys thirteen months apart *is* exciting and adventurous. Every day they learn something new, I learn something new, and I go to bed knowing that my job as a stay-at-home mom is a blessing because not everyone can do that job.

Life Lesson:
What is ordinary to you is extraordinary to someone else.

23
One More Try

In the late '60s, Elton John was just starting to make a name for himself in England. Previous attempts to become "known" in the United States had failed. His producer at the time, Dick James, decided to have one more last-ditch effort for a concert tour in the U.S. at the Troubadour Club in Los Angeles, California. Dick James send Elton's album to the club manager and he booked Elton for a six-night run at the club.

Fortunately for Elton, there were many famous people in the audience that night, many of them astounded by this little-known piano player's talent. It was this last-ditch effort that launched Elton's career in the United States.

There here have been many times in my life in which God gave His last-ditch effort to get me to follow the plan He created for me. I have struggled with that my entire life—trying to follow what I wanted to do and not listening to God. Time and time again, I try to make things go my way, and time and time again, God shows me His way. Despite my best efforts to ignore His plan, He has never, ever given up on me.

As I reflect on the times when I recognized God's efforts, I see this happened in threes. I'd like to say it happened that way because of the religious significance of the number three, but that's not the case. It happened in threes because I didn't listen the first two times. That third time was God's last-ditch effort. Fortunately for me, I listened after that third time and saw for myself the plan He wanted me to follow.

I see now that it was God's plan for us to become debt-free. My first lesson was in not being able to go to Elton's sixtieth birthday concert in 2007. The next lesson was when my friend Katrina told me about Dave Ramsey's Financial Peace University course. Even as I saw her excitement over the positive changes in her life, I didn't listen. Finally, in December 2009, I clearly heard the voice in my head say, "This is totally wrong. You have lost the true meaning of Christmas."

How did we pay off over $43,500 of consumer debt in less than four years? We followed the plan, remained diligent to the process, and, by the grace of God, made it happen.

You'd think I would have learned from that example, as well as the countless other number of times God finally got through to me and I gave in to His plan.

Yes, you would think. Have I mentioned that I'm stubborn?

One of the best examples of my stubbornness to what God wanted me to do happened in late 2012. By this time, we were fully involved in budgeting, saving, and paying off debt. We had set the goal to be debt-free by September 2013. I was teaching coupon workshops and helping people create a budget. Things were good; we were in a good place. I wasn't looking for anything different. But God had other plans.

I was teaching a coupon workshop at my friend Holly's house. By this time, my workshop had evolved into a PowerPoint presentation and worksheets the participants could use as a guide. About halfway through the workshop, Holly suddenly exclaimed, "Okay, stop!" She said it in such a way that caught me off guard. Of course, I stopped.

"Do you have time after this workshop to talk?" she asked.

"Yes," I hesitantly replied, "I can."

"Okay, great," she said, "You can continue," and she smiled.

That was weird. I knew Holly well enough that if she asked to talk to me afterward, I should do it. Holly was an entrepreneur and a business owner. I finished up the workshop and when everyone left, we sat down to talk.

Holly told me that it was obvious how passionate I was about helping people. She proceeded to tell me that, in her opinion, I was charging too little for the workshops and I needed to start my own business. I needed to help people with more than just learning to coupon.

Oh, okay. I had no interest in doing anything she suggested. I didn't want to be a business owner or an entrepreneur. I didn't have a business degree, I didn't know how to start a business, and I certainly didn't know how to write a business plan. My entire working life I had always worked for other people—or did I?

When I was in high school, I had my own dog sitting and babysitting service. I was an entrepreneur then and didn't even realize it. But now I am an adult and have adult responsibilities. I am a wife and a mom; how do I have time to create and run a business?

I had worked for small business owners before, and you know what I saw? When they weren't sleeping (and that wasn't a lot to begin with), they were working on their businesses. They had no time to do anything else. I wasn't at a point in my life in which I wanted the business to take over my life. But, I respected Holly and appreciated her input, so while I didn't immediately act on her advice, I didn't completely discount it, either.

A few months after my conversation with Holly, someone else mentioned to me during a coupon workshop that I was *really* good at what I was doing and I should start a business. I gave it some thought. My end-of-workshop evaluations were always positive. More people requested I teach workshops. The feedback I got from workshop participants who were putting into practice what they learned was great.

In many ways, it made sense for me to start my own company. I could set my own hours and my own pay. I would have the freedom to work when and where I wanted. Both boys were in school during the day now, so I could work then. I could work some evenings and some weekends if needed. I found myself beginning to consider the possibility, but I wasn't quite ready to commit. But, God always had a plan.

I am a huge fan of Notre Dame football. My husband bought me a copy of Rudy Ruettiger's autobiography, *Rudy*, for my birthday in September that year, but I didn't get around to reading it until late October. Rudy spent his entire life dreaming about playing football for Notre Dame. A tragic event was the propelling force behind him leaving home to pursue this dream. Eventually, he made it into Notre Dame and was chosen to be on the practice squad for the football team. Through a series of events, he was finally allowed to play in his last game as a senior. He sacked the quarterback and was carried off the field. Since that game, no other Notre Dame football player had ever been carried off the field. As a fan of football and a fan of Notre Dame, I loved reading this story. However, the book is not just about football or Notre Dame. It's ultimately a story of perseverance.

I don't know for certain, but I would imagine that since that day, no player had worked as hard or overcome as many obstacles as Rudy. He not only pursued his dream, but he was persistent in his endeavor. He overcame many trials and never, ever gave up. The book goes into detail, too, of the many obstacles he had to overcome to make the movie. In the latter part of the book, he writes:

"I encourage everyone I know to share his or her success stories with anyone who'll listen. Not just to share the end result—bragging won't help anyone—but to share the process. That's the key: tell them how you did it. Tell them how you

achieved your success. Show them that wherever there's a will, there's a way. Open their eyes to the possibilities in their own lives. You never know whose life you'll change."

I remember lying in bed one night reading that, and it just felt heavy. I needed to stop reading and go to sleep. When I awoke the next morning, my very first thought was, *start your business*. Normally, my very first thought is, *go make coffee*, so I just knew this was God's voice in my head. Never had I felt such a conviction to start my business. And then, I realized this was the third time He'd tried to get my attention. God had tried to show me the way through a workshop participant, through Holly, and finally through my husband, who purchased *Rudy*. There is no way that God's hand was not guiding that entire process.

Since Holly had previously offered to help me start the business, I called her and told her the news. The first thing she asked me was, "When do you plan on starting your business?" I had not even given this a thought. Not one minute was spent formulating a plan before I'd called her.

I didn't have an answer, but found myself saying, "Well, I guess on January 1, because that's when everyone decides to start New Year's resolutions," I answered.

"January 1 of next year?" she asked.

I realized she meant fourteen months away and quickly thought that was too much time.

I said, "No, as in January 1, 2012."

Holly exclaimed, "But that's in less than two months!"

"I know, but I have to start it then. Waiting fourteen months is too far away and the timing is right to start it January 1."

Crazy. That's what I am. Who was I to think that in less than two months I could launch a company? I had no business experience, no experience working for myself, and no idea where to begin. What if I failed? What if I wasn't good enough? But, I knew I was supposed to do this. I had to make it happen. When I talked to my husband about it, I could tell he wasn't too sure about the idea. This wasn't the first time I was crazy about doing something and hadn't followed through. This time, though, was different. I had this crazy idea to get us out of debt, and that was working. So, I used that as my example, instead of all the other failed attempts. We decided that I would take some money out of savings for basic startup costs: a website, some business cards, and office supplies.

If I was going to do this, I had to be all in. I had to be an official business entity. To me, this is the least favorite of all business activities—filing for an LLC and obtaining a tax ID number. How boring is filling out paperwork? But, it had to be done. I needed a business name. I started out as: 1410 Endeavors, LLC, dba Money Mojo.

The LLC name comes from 1 Timothy 4:10, "That is why we labor and strive, because we have put our hope in the living God, who is the Savior of all people, and especially of those who believe," and *Money Mojo* was just a name I created. My tagline was something like, "Creating Money Magic," or something like that. I was so proud of myself for such a clever name. However, *Money Mojo* wasn't very well received, despite my best attempts at marketing. (Keep in mind, I had no idea how to be a marketing department).

I met with a group of business people from an organization called SCORE. This organization helps people like me develop a business plan and learn how to be a business owner. Two of the things I remember most from that meeting were: my business name wouldn't work, and I needed to go back to school to get a certification of some sort. Okay, I could sort of understand the first directive, but given I had already spent hours trying to come up with a business name, I wasn't going to try to change it at that point. And why did I need to go back to school? Because according to the people at SCORE, no one would hire me based on the fact I only had "life experience."

Yes, my basic premise for why people would hire me as their coach was because I had "been there, done that." I wanted to help the people who were like us, living paycheck-to-paycheck, deep in debt, no plans for their financial future, and were stressed, worried, and anxious about money. I had no special degrees or certifications.

I went into my meeting at SCORE feeling excited about starting a business, and I left with the idea that I had no business starting a business. But, I knew this was what I was supposed to do and I needed a plan. Looking back, I realize that my meeting at SCORE was really above my head. Not that the people there weren't helpful, but it was more than what I needed at that time. I just wasn't in a place where I was ready or wanted to learn all the "business" stuff behind owning a business. I just wanted to help people, and my background in teaching had already prepared me for that.

On the way home from the meeting, I was listening to *The Dave Ramsey Show* on the radio. This was something I did often while in the car, but it was the first time I heard something different—an advertisement for Dave Ramsey Counselor Training. That was it! There was my answer! I would go to Dave Ramsey Counselor Training and that would fulfill the need to be certified to do what I wanted to do.

I thought when I launched on January 1, I wouldn't get a call from my first client until well after the New Year, so I could use the in-between time to learn how to do what I needed to do. It was a totally risky move because I knew if someone called me on that day, I wouldn't be ready—or so I thought. I know now that I would have been ready; all I had to do was teach what I knew how to do. I knew how to teach and I knew how to budget; I just did not have the confidence to believe that someone would pay me. However, the overwhelming response to launching my business on social media was, "It's about time," so I knew I was at least headed in the right direction.

Life Lesson:
When people speak, listen.

24
Moving Forward

My first client meeting happened just weeks after launch, at the end of January. I attended Dave Ramsey Counselor Training in February 2012. That training taught me more about how to deal with people and their situations than just about budgeting. Yes, we did learn about that, but I also learned that dealing with money is more than just dealing with the math; it's a very emotional experience. Therefore, it's so hard for people to "get right" with money.

As part of the training, we were taught by the people who work for Dave Ramsey. These people taught us based on their previous experience and their current experience. They have coached hundreds of people. I had learned from my previous direct sales job that if you want to do what someone else does, you do exactly what they do. So, I took copious numbers of notes and took advantage of every opportunity to learn while I was there.

The best experience came on day three or four of the conference when we were divided into smaller groups and took a tour of Dave Ramsey's office, Financial Peace Plaza. It is there where the daily radio show is conducted. I don't recall an experience quite like I had at Counselor Training. It was located outside of Nashville, Tennessee, so while Southern hospitality is expected, everyone exudes that spirit and I felt genuinely welcomed. Dave Ramsey has created a corporate culture where everyone is happy and truly loves the work that they do. Many of the employees told me how blessed they feel to work there and be a part of the organization. It was very much an atmosphere of warmth and welcoming.

As part of the tour, we were taken into the main lobby. The walls there are covered with the names of people who have traveled to Financial Peace Plaza to give their Debt-Free Scream on the radio show. It was amazing and inspiring to read each name, how much debt they had paid off, and how long it took them to do so. I decided that when we paid off our mortgage, we would take a family trip and do the same. What an experience that would be!

There was a large glass window divider in the lobby separating the main lobby from Dave's radio studio, where we could watch him do his show. I was so excited to meet the man who created the program that saved our financial life. Efficiency was the name of the game here, because he only had the amount of time during the commercial break to come out and meet us. We were placed in a line, told to hand our camera to the person in line behind us, and instructed to come forward to meet Dave, shake hands, say hello, and then move out of the way for the next person. This must go fast so everyone gets a turn.

As trainees, we suspected we'd have an opportunity to meet Dave, so I'd brought my copy of his book, *EntreLeadership*, with me on the off-chance I would actually meet him. Once I arrived at the training, it was confirmed that a meet-and-greet was part of the session. I was so glad I brought my book, but because our directions were to say hello, shake hands, get a picture, and move out of the way, I wasn't sure he'd sign it for me. I am generally not one to go against the directive given, but I also did not want to miss out on the opportunity.

My Elton concert experiences had taught me to be persistent without getting in trouble, so I drew on that and formulated a plan. I was going to follow the direction and then loop back to the end of the line to get my autograph. I had to take the chance that there would still be time, but I would have felt awful if my asking for an autograph during my turn would have prevented someone else from meeting him.

There we were in line when Dave Ramsey walked out into the lobby. A female employee directed us, and we each get our turn to meet Dave and take our picture with him. I told him how honored I was to be at Counselor Training and thanked him for creating FPU. His reply was so humble and genuine as he simply said, "Oh no, thank *you* for being here."

And, yes, I was able to go to the back and get his autograph!

Life Lesson:
Down-to-earth. Humble. Welcoming. Genuine.
No matter how big my business grows,
remember to be those things.

25
Living the Life

I had successfully filled the time in between concert runs. Aside from being a wife and a mom, I added *entrepreneur* to my list of titles. Life was hectic and crazy, and I loved every minute of it! I was only three months into running my business and still about a year away from becoming debt-free, but that didn't stop me from pursuing my dream. I hadn't gotten this far to let life stand in my way. When the opportunity arose to attend three concerts, three nights in a row, in three different cities, I was ready for the challenge of pulling it off.

The first city on the tour would bring us back to the site where Valerie and I first met; the second was the city where I attended my first concert; and the last was the city where I met my friend, Tommy. We were in the front row for all three of those concerts. I was a good student and had learned the tricks of the trade by this point. I had accomplished the task alone, and was so excited. The 2Cellos were touring with Elton John and the band, and it was one of the few times Elton John had allowed another group to not only open for him, but provide additional accompaniment through the concert.

For this trip, Valerie and I would attend all three concerts together, but we'd drive separately. There was a strategy to this arrangement. It was my job to get tickets. To get the best seats, it was imperative for me to be in the right place at the right time. I am an early-rising, get-up-and-go person. I can go from my bed to the shower and out the door in thirty minutes or less. Valerie does not possess this enthusiasm for the early morning hours.

It would be by the grace of God, my ability to be in the right place at the right time, and the knowledge about the ticket-buying process I had acquired from Valerie that for each concert, I was able to get front-row seats. The consistency of sitting in the front row would become important at the second of the three shows in Raleigh, where I decided at the last minute to grab a marker and a piece of printer paper and make a sign reading, "THIS IS MY 20th SHOW (please sign my ticket!)." I had not one, but two exciting experiences in Raleigh—one because I knew my stuff, and two because I improvised communication.

I always arrive early for the shows, more than an hour before the doors even open. I can't stand the idea of being late. I also get incredibly anxious; I don't want to miss out on anything, so I always arrive early.

Such was the case for this show. I arrived early and, while standing around the area where the line would form, I met up with Carol and Joe, whom I had met at previous concerts through Valerie. We chatted a while and, as lines began to form, I chose one and found my place to wait. The doors opened and we all moved into the venue. Once there, I found an entrance into the arena and joined in with the line of people.

Being married to a Marine has taught me to always be astutely aware of my surroundings. Although I'm not always great at doing so, for whatever reason, I was on top of it that night while in line, constantly scanning the crowd, becoming aware of the people around me, and waiting my turn to move into the venue. At the entrance, the usher stopped each person to ask if they needed assistance finding their seats. I noticed a young girl with an older woman (I assumed her grandmother) in line in front of me. As the usher asks her if she needed help, I heard her say, "Oh, no. I know where I'm going. I'm going to meet my dad. He's the drummer for the band."

She said it with such confidence and conviction the usher believed her and let her on her way. I quickly informed the usher that I knew where I was going (with the same confidence and conviction) and was also sent on my way. Oh, yes, I knew where I was going—right behind that girl who was just steps away.

Once I got behind her, I leaned forward and very sarcastically said, "Wow! That was a great line! No way your dad is Nigel Olsson."

She stopped, turned toward me, and said, "Yes, he is. Do you know my dad?"

"Well, only if you count me as a huge fan of Elton and the band, and this is my twentieth concert! Nigel is your dad? Are you really going to meet him?"

"Yes," she answered.

The next words flew out of my mouth before I could even think about them: "Can I come with you?"

She hesitated for a second and then said, "Sure! Come on!"

I couldn't believe what was happening, but there was no time to process. We walked forward and down the stairs to the floor level. Just before we were stopped by another usher, she asked my name.

"Melissa," I replied.

The usher stopped us and she said, "Hi! We are going there," and pointed to an opening in the hallway. "This is my friend Melissa and she's coming with us."

To my surprise, the usher allowed us all to go. We walked to the end of the hallway and another usher pulled back the curtain. There he was, standing at the end of the hallway: Nigel Olsson!

We walked forward; I was last in line. Nigel greeted the older woman. The younger woman introduced me. "This is my friend, Melissa."

I wasn't sure what to do, so I said, "Hello, Mr. Olsson, it's an honor to meet you." As he thanked me for coming to the concert, I was struck by how soft-spoken he was. I also noticed his strong British accent, much stronger than I expected.

He told our group that we'd be going upstairs. I had no idea what was happening upstairs and wasn't sure I was included, but soon the young woman said to me, "Come on, you can come, too."

I followed them up a flight of stairs where an usher stopped us. There was some discussion, which ended with Nigel saying we were all going with him. We continued down a long hallway to a room filled with people. When we entered the room, Nigel asked me to stay near the entrance, so I did. A quick scan of the room indicated there were several bar tables with stools and some long buffet tables with food along the back wall. The room was full of people. I didn't recognize anyone until I saw Davey Johnstone sitting at a table, talking to some people. He could not have been more than fifteen feet away from me.

After a few minutes, Nigel returned and told me I would have to leave because I didn't have a pass. I told him it was not a problem and asked for an autograph, which he happily gave me. I found my new friend standing a few feet away and walked over to her to thank her and explain the situation. She was apologetic, but I assured her it was not a problem. Oh, how I did not want to leave, but I also did not want to be escorted out of that room and out of the building, so I made my way back down the hallway, down the stairs, and to my seat.

You can imagine my friends' surprise when I finally showed up at our seats. They had been wondering what happened to me. As I told them what had happened, I still couldn't believe it myself.

At some point, either before the concert or during, I decided to make a sign, hold it up during the concert, and try to see who I could get to sign my ticket. This concert tour included a full house (per se) of musical guests—the back-up singers (Tata Vega, Rose Stone, Lisa Stone, and Jean Witherspoon), the 2Cellos (Luka Sulic and Stjepan Hauser), and the band members. Our seats were directly in front of the 2Cellos—easy enough for me to get their attention. Throughout the concert, I held up my sign. I didn't really expect anyone from the stage to autograph it for me, even though I did want someone to sign it, and it was getting closer to the end of the show.

I made eye contact with Luka, showed him my sign, and made a signing motion in the air with my pen. He nodded and jerked his head toward the end of the stage. I knew that meant he would meet me there after the set. I nodded in agreement and quickly glanced over to the side of the stage. The entrance to the backstage area was blocked off by two security guards. I wasn't exactly sure how this was going to work, but I knew it had to.

Once Luka and Stjepan were done playing, they began to walk to the stairs on the side of the stage and I started my walk to the blocked-off area. I got as close as I could before the security guard blocked my way and, drawing on previous experience with security guards, I very calmly and nicely said, "It's ok, the guys are coming to see me; look!" As he turned to look, the 2Cellos were walking toward the gated area, so I leaned up on the five-foot-tall speaker and placed my ticket there with my marker. They managed to get on the other side of the speaker and I shouted, "Thank you!" to them while they both took turns signing my ticket. They each thanked me for coming to the show and asked my name before the moment was over. Other fans saw what was happening and rushed to my spot, so Luka and Stjepan had to leave in a hurry to avoid the chaos. It wasn't until I was back in my hotel room that I noticed they had personalized their autographs, just for me.

Life Lesson:

Speak up and communicate! Improvise communication when needed. People cannot read your mind.

26
The Unforgettable Moment

In the summer of 2013, Jack and I were nearing the end of our debt-free journey. I received a phone call from Valerie.

"Elton John is doing a concert in D.C. and one in Atlanta. Do you want to go?"

I hesitated a minute, dreading the answer to the following question, "When are they?"

"Not until November," she answered.

"November?" I did some quick math in my head and exclaimed, "Yes! I can go!"

Valerie was a little taken aback, "What? Are you sure? You don't have to think about it? You don't have to see if you can get money together?"

"No, I can go! We'll be debt-free at the end of September and there will be at least two paychecks between that and the time of the concert; I can go!"

I'll never forget that moment. I had progressed from missing out on a concert because I didn't have money, to going to concerts once I scraped the money together, to being able to say yes without a lot of thought because the money would be available for me to go. The only problem was that I didn't have the money to buy tickets when they went on sale, months before the concert. *Not a problem*, I thought, *I'll get them later*.

After working through the different travel scenarios, I decided to fly from North Carolina to Washington, D.C., then from D.C. to Atlanta, and then fly from Atlanta back home after the show. Something came up with Valerie and she couldn't attend the D.C. show, but my friends Tommy and Doug were going to that show, too, so I wasn't going to be alone.

I made plans knowing that we were on track to be debt-free by my fortieth birthday. Valerie called me in the summer and my birthday was in September. I knew that Jack and I had planned a weeklong vacation in the mountains in early October and that, since the concert wasn't until November, I didn't have to book a flight until mid-October. The logistics were all working out. Everything was falling into place; debt-free at the end of September, vacation in October, go see Elton in November.

My flight did not arrive until the afternoon of the day of the concert. While I traveled, Tommy was on ticket duty. I had met Tommy at the Richmond concert when he approached me and said, "Hello, RocketmanFan!" I was a little taken aback and he said, "That *is* your car in the parking lot with the license plate, right?" Oh! Yes, there weren't many cars in the parking lot, and once again, my license plate gave me the opportunity to meet a new friend. After that concert, we agreed to stay in touch and ended up attending this same show.

By the time I arrived at the venue, it was mid-afternoon and he did not have good news. There were tickets available, but they were not great seats. That wasn't the news I wanted to hear, but I agreed to take over for a while. I was tired from traveling but could feel the adrenaline starting to kick in. It was hours until concert time and the venue was alive with activity.

I settled in with my luggage and my phone for a while, and Tommy went back to the hotel. When he returned, I went to the hotel and he resumed ticket duty. It was almost 6:00 p.m. before I got my second-row ticket, thanks to Tommy. Without his help, this never would have happened.

I learned a very valuable lesson that day. Never, ever go to a concert without a ticket in hand. The concert was nearly sold out and, as always, Elton put on a great show. I could get up to the stage to get an autograph; Elton signed my copy of his book, *Love is the Cure*.

I had one day of travel in between the D.C. and Atlanta concerts. This was a blessing because my flight from D.C. to Atlanta was canceled and I did not end up arriving in Atlanta until almost 8:00 p.m., which was show time the following evening. Good thing I didn't have a concert to go to that night, or else I may have ended up being one of those irate airline passengers.

The next day—concert day—I walked from my hotel to the CNN Center and concert venue. I had a little bit of time to tour the CNN Center and do a quick walk through Centennial Park. There was not, however, time to go to the Georgia Aquarium or the Coca-Cola Museum. I probably could have made time, but that would have meant missing out on time at the concert venue. I'd hate to miss out on an opportunity because I was sight-seeing. Valerie arrived later in the day and we met up with Jenny, another Elton fan whom Valerie has known for a long time.

We had no luck getting better seats, so Valerie and I were in the twelfth row for this show. She'd purchased them during the Ticketmaster sale and we were so happy to be that close. We found out the concert was sold out; tickets were hard to get because this was a special event concert since Atlanta, Georgia, is Elton John's American hometown. There were so many family and friends of Elton's and the band at that concert; there was no way we were going to get closer than twelfth row.

The energy at this concert was off the charts. There was a huge difference between the crowd at the D.C. concert and the crowd in Atlanta. It was non-stop dancing the entire night, and Elton fed off the energy of the crowd.

Upon arriving home, I was overwhelmed by two things.

One, I had flown to two concerts in three days, and two, I had cash-flowed the entire trip. Concerts twenty-three and twenty-four were in the books, and I discovered the very beginning of what debt-free life would look like.

Life Lesson:
Money is a tool to pursue your dreams, not an obstacle that should stand in your way. Money allows you to say "yes" to opportunities.

27
We're Debt-Free!

When I started Financial Peace University, my goal was to become debt-free. Initially, I didn't set a timeline. It seemed too overwhelming to determine a debt-free date. However, the more I progressed on our budget and saw our debt snowball plan working, I knew I needed a deadline.

I decided I wanted to be debt-free by the time I turned forty.

In total, that gave us three years, eight months, and twenty-seven days to pay off $43,544 of debt. If I had set that goal when we first started the process, I would have told you it was impossible. But with hope and diligence to the process comes success.

At the time of our journey, *The Dave Ramsey Show* was on the local radio station and I listened to it every day while picking up the boys from school. One day, they were in the car when someone had called in to do their debt-free scream. I listened intently until we heard Dave Ramsey say, "Okay, count it down!" and the people would scream, "Three, two, one—We're Debt-Freeeeeeeeeeeeeeeeeeeeeeee!"

The sounds of applause and Dave Ramsey congratulating them came through the radio speakers, and the boys' interest was piqued. One them turned to me and said, "Mommy, when are we going to be 'dead-free?'"

"Did you say *dead?*"

"Yes," he replied.

"There's no such thing as *dead-free.* Do you mean *debt-free?*"

"Well, whatever those people were all excited about," he replied.

"Oh yes, they are *debt*-free; that means they paid off all of their debt," I explained.

"Oh, we are doing that, right Mommy?"

"Yes, we are," I replied.

"Can we call and do our scream too?"

"Yes, we can."

And, in that moment, I was committed to making it happen. I called *The Dave Ramsey Show* to let them know we would be calling them on my fortieth birthday to do our debt-free scream. I was congratulated and told we should schedule that no more than six weeks out. They wanted to be sure we were going to be debt-free when we called. I understood that. I made a note to call back and schedule later.

On September 27, 2013, we made the last payment to Sallie Mae. We'd paid off $43,544 of consumer debt; six credit cards, two vehicle loans, and my student loan. We called in to *The Dave Ramsey Show* later that afternoon to do our debt-free scream. The boys participated and, to this day, I get a little emotional when I listen to that recording. It was such a defining moment in our lives; the boys were officially the first generation on either side of our family to know a life of handling money God's way. They know "debt is dumb" and they know we save for what we want and buy what we need. This moment in time, everything we did to get there and everything we do going forward is our legacy to them.

Life Lesson:
Moments will define your legacy. Make sure they are moments to remember.

28
Personality Flaw

I have a habit of jumping into something before I know that whole picture. That's just a flaw of my personality; jump in to the deep end and figure out how to get to the shallow end before drowning. There's a song by Elton John in which the lyrics challenge us to take risks. I don't remember now what live stream concert I was listening to, but I clearly remember sitting in the back bedroom of our house—before it was the boys' bedroom—sitting at the desk, wearing my headphones, and watching the live stream concert.

Elton John had written a new album and was debuting some songs from it. Obviously, as a huge fan, I know I am going to love every new song he writes and that is true, but some I do love more than others.

As soon as he hit the opening notes of "The Bridge," I thought, "Oh! I love this song!" I had not heard a single lyric, but almost immediately, the music drew me in and I felt a connection to it in my soul. Then, the lyrics—oh, the lyrics! Bernie Taupin is a masterful lyricist. Elton John is a master composer of just the right notes and tempo to match the lyrics. If you have never heard this song before, search for it on YouTube. It is inspirational, beautiful, and just musically perfect in every way. Of course, that's my opinion; but seriously, it is one of my most favorite Elton John songs.

At some point in my life, I had to decide that I wanted more than an ordinary life. I had to decide for myself what I wanted for me, despite what others had in mind for me. My life was created by God and I should be following His plan. I didn't always believe that my goals and dreams were given to me by God, but now I do. There have been too many uncanny coincidences that have happened to give anything other than God the credit. At some point, I had to make that decision to cross the bridge from where I was to where I wanted to be:

I wanted to be a better wife.

I wanted to be a better mom.

I wanted to be a successful entrepreneur.

I wanted to stop letting money run my life.

I wanted to be a better friend and family member.

I wanted to help more people, inspire more people, and make my life one that had meaning and left a legacy.

All of that and more, because my strong, type-A personality and "this is it" isn't good enough for me. I had to make things work; I had to prove people wrong. I had to live the life I wanted to live and not the life other people expected me to live.

Social pressures are not an easy thing to go against. Everyone has an opinion about where you fit in, what your life should look like, and who you are to be with. When we spend too much time listening to those voices and not enough time listening to our own inner voice, we live a life of turmoil. That daily battle against who we truly want to be and who are trying to measure up to be is exhausting.

It is only in coming to terms with who we want to be that we are really, truly ourselves and can begin to take the steps toward crossing that bridge to the life we want. It sounds drastic, I know, but to get what we want out of life, we must be willing to take huge risks.

"When will you give up?"

"How many times are you going to keep going? What's that number you are trying to achieve?"

These are the most common questions people ask when I say, "My dream is to meet Elton John." Of course, it seems like a crazy, impossible dream, but it's my dream. Years ago, I decided I was going to pursue it, no matter what. However, I realized that at some point, I had to step out of my comfort zone and do things a little differently. I had to live up to those lyrics and risk it all, even if it meant tapping into my edgy, non-conservative side.

I just needed a little bit of help. And I knew just where to ask for it.

Life Lesson:
Pursing a dream involves taking a risk. Take that risk.

29
Friends

In the summer of 2014, I made a solo road trip to Charlestown, West Virginia, and then to Charlotte, North Carolina, to attend my twenty-fifth and twenty-sixth concerts. I was meeting friends at the concerts, but we were not traveling together. I was excited that Tommy and Doug were going to both shows and I was going to meet some of their friends, too. I love making new friends, especially Elton fans. It was at these concerts where I first heard Elton's plans to play a concert at the Barclay Center in Brooklyn, New York, on New Year's Eve. I did not hesitate in making my decision to go. This was going to be an epic adventure and a once-in-a-lifetime experience that I was not going to miss. I'd find a way to make it happen.

I needed a new outfit for the occasion. This was a special event and I needed something special. Some backstory — I belong to a Facebook group with women from all over the country. This group is a subgroup of another Facebook group, of which I became a member when I answered a tweet from author Jon Acuff asking for people to join him on an adventure. That was it. I had no idea what the adventure was or where we were going or what we were going to do, but I did know about Jon Acuff. I assumed he wasn't going to anything too crazy or absurd. I assumed that since Jon Acuff was associated with Dave Ramsey and Dave Ramsey was a pretty smart, laid back kind of guy, that whatever adventure Jon was asking us to join was something I could participate in.

I answered without fully understanding what I was getting myself into. I answered the only way I normally do anything new in my life—I jump in the deep end head-first and figure out how to get to the shallow end, to solid footing, to not having to tread or hold my head above the water. No plan, no direction, no sense of hesitation.

It was June 2013. At this point in my life, we were three months away from becoming debt-free. My business was six months old. I was beginning to believe that I could do all the things I had dreamed of doing. I was twenty-two concerts into pursuing my dream. Why not join this great adventure?

Making that one decision totally changed the way I think about going after and achieving the things I dreamed about. I learned it's not just enough to dream and say you have a goal; you must create and follow actionable steps. You must build the path that leads you to your *big* dream. That group of people that Jon Acuff collected? They all have *big* dreams—*and* they all create the actionable steps to build the path toward achieving that dream. That is the difference. That is exactly what I needed to learn more about. I was still new to the process and even at that, I wasn't creating my own process. Up until this point, I was following a proven process that worked by following the steps outlined in Financial Peace University. I was doing what I was told. I wasn't taking a lot of chances or risks. I wasn't laying it all out on the line and seeing what happened. I was playing it safe. I was ready to change. I accepted the invitation, and that is what led me to my women-only Facebook group.

You should know that clothes shopping is not one of my special gifts, nor is it something I enjoy. I don't have a sense of what's "in" or "out" in terms of style. I tend to buy what I like and prefer mix-and-match over having several dozen outfits. My wardrobe basically consists of jeans, shorts (almost Bermudalength but not quite that long), polo shirts (some with stripes, but mostly solids), two pairs of khaki pants, long-sleeve, button-down collared shirts, three pairs of Doc Marten shoes, and four pairs of Converse sneakers. I have white, "no show" socks and knee-length striped or argyle style socks in different colors, but that's it. I have some t-shirts too, but they are mostly ones I have collected from conferences or through my volunteer work with fundraisers for Canines for Service.

You can see why I needed some help. Nothing I owned was going to work for this big event. I was going to see Elton John on New Year's Eve at The Barclay Center in Brooklyn, New York. I needed something different. Something that was still "me," but totally *not* me. This event called for leaping outside of my comfort zone, taking a big risk with my clothing choice, and it had to be an outfit that stood out.

"I need some help," I posted. "I need a shirt that is my style, but is also a 'seeing Elton John on New Year's Eve' shirt."

Within minutes of posting my request, I had suggestions and links to different shirts. People were asking questions to get a better idea of what I wanted. We were throwing around ideas in the comment section of the post. I was clicking links and answering questions, believing that someone, somewhere would know just where I could find the right shirt. My friend Julianne posted a link and I opened it. It was the right style but wow, it was something I would totally never wear. My initial reaction was, "Oh no, no way." But something stopped me from dismissing it entirely. After all, it was the right style—a long-sleeve, button-down, collared shirt. The price wasn't outrageous, either. I could order it online and have it sent to the house (my favorite part of clothes shopping!).

What was holding me back? The material—the entire shirt was covered in little silver sequins. Little silver sequins are not and have never been in any part of my wardrobe, ever. They exude "girly-girl," and that is totally not me.

But, it did fit the "going to see Elton John on NYE" requirement and it was my style, so I ordered it. When it arrived, I was excited. I pulled it out of the bag to show my husband, exclaiming, "Look at my new shirt!" to which he replied, "Wow! It's entirely see-through."

What?

Now, *that* is totally not my style at all. No way am I going to wear a shirt that is completely see-through. And this was exactly that. Each little silver sequin was glued onto a see-through mesh style fabric, and so the little slivers of gap in between each circle were enough to create a see-through shirt. I need help again, so I went back to posting in the group:

"I ordered the shirt and I love it, but it's see through. How do I fix that? What do I do?"

"You buy a camisole."

"A what?

"A camisole. It's like a bra but longer, and you don't wear a bra underneath that. You just wear the camisole and then put your shirt on over it."

"Okay, where do I get this camisole? What store carries them? What color should I get?"

"Any store will have them in the lingerie department. Black, you should get a black camisole."

Great. Not only do I now own a see-through, silver-sequined, sparkly shirt, but now I must physically walk into a store, find a camisole, try it on, and purchase that, too. Fantastic.

I told you I wasn't a girly-girl. But, thanks to help from my friends, I had a direction. I knew where I had to go and what I had to buy, and it solved my problem.

(Even amid writing this story, I had to call my friend, Carla, and ask her to help me remember the word *camisole* because I couldn't remember what that piece of clothing was called.)

This was going to be my twenty-seventh Elton John concert, and only the third time I'd seen him in the New York City area. It had been almost six months since I had been to a concert and I was so excited for this one, mainly because our New Year's Eve celebrations consist of struggling to stay awake until midnight. We just aren't the "going-out" type of people.

I decided I didn't want to fly up to New York to attend the concert and then fly home. I was concerned about the weather and traveling during that time of the year. I wanted to play it safe and fly up a few days before the concert. If everything went well with the weather, I would have a few days to explore New York City, and if it didn't, I had plenty of time to deal with delayed flights and not miss out on this epic adventure.

Here was the plan:

Fly to NYC.

Stay a few days with my female friend Dale in Manhattan.

Visit my college friend, Tubbs, while I was there.

Take the Subway to Brooklyn and meet up with Tommy and Doug.

Attend the concert, stay at the hotel close to The Barclay Center, and fly home the next day.

I had an outfit and a plan. I knew I bought a concert ticket prior to my trip, but I couldn't remember now where my seat was. It didn't matter, though, because thanks to Tommy, I ended up with a second-row ticket.

At some point during the planning process, Tommy told me that backstage tour passes were available for purchase for the concert. I knew a little bit about the backstage tour from posts in the Facebook groups for Elton fans. Everyone who posted about it said it was totally worth the money and such a great experience. Tommy and Doug were taking the tour, so I decided that I would, too. I knew it wouldn't give me the chance to meet Elton John in person—it wasn't a ticket for a meet and greet—but I also knew that taking a backstage tour would put me in a position for a chance meeting. At the very least, it gave me an opportunity to get one step closer to my dream.

I'm all in for this concert. Flights, hotels, concert ticket, new outfit, and a backstage pass tour. A potential once-in-a-lifetime opportunity that I was not going to miss out on this time. An Elton John concert in Brooklyn, New York, on New Year's Eve is just not something that happens every year. Being debt-free allowed me the option to take advantage of this opportunity.

One of the greatest things about the backstage tour is that it isn't a tour of the backstage, but a tour of what's on the stage—the set and the instruments. The physical stage, the digital backdrop, and the multi-bulb chandelier, as well as all the speakers, wires, sound board, and everything else needed to make the concert experience what it is to the tour. Everything is shipped in on eighteen-wheelers in large crates or travel boxes. Here are a few interesting pieces of trivia.

The soundboard is analog. There is an actual person adjusting the sound throughout the concert. There are different sets of the same instruments because sometimes the logistics work out that they cannot transport one set straight from one concert to another. So, the sets "leapfrog" from one venue to the next.

Elton John has several pianos. There are five black pianos named Aretha, Diana, Nina, Kay, and Winifred. The red piano is named Nikita. Blossom is also known as The Million Dollar Piano, which he uses for his Vegas shows. Each one is named after a famous person who has musically inspired Elton; for example, Aretha Franklin, Diana Krall, and Nina Simone. The black concert tour pianos are all original harp pianos, not digital.

During the tour, we were given a historical and technical history about everything involved in the production of a concert. We started at the back, at the sound board, and worked our way up the side aisle to the side of the stage. At any other time, this would be an off-limits area, as it is the first part of being backstage. We ascended the same set of stairs that Elton uses during the concert and there we were, standing on the stage. Elton's piano was just a few feet away; it's so close I could touch it if I wanted to, and I did want to. It's not just any piano; it's Elton John's piano. Right there, just feet away from me and the rest of the group.

Our tour guide took us around to each set of instruments—Jon Mahon's percussion drum kit, Nigel Olsson's drum kit, Kim Bullard's keyboard kit—and explained some history of each musician, as well as the different uses of each instrument for different songs. As we finished that part of the tour, the guide announced, "And, last but not least, the piano," and proceeded to give a history of it, including some more trivia-type information that fascinated everyone in our group—die-hard fans of all things Elton John. Finally, the guide spoke these words: "If you all will form a line, you can go sit at the piano and I'll take your picture."

What? Did he just actually say we can sit at Elton John's piano?

"You cannot play or touch the piano, but you can sit there and I'll take your picture. We'll check to make sure it's good, and then we'll move on to the next person. We have to move quickly, but I want to be sure you have a good picture, too."

Sometimes I don't hear so well. I have partial hearing loss in my right ear from standing against one of the large stage speakers at the concert in Charleston, South Carolina, in 2007. As I have gotten older, the hearing loss has become more bothersome. Sometimes, in a noisy environment, I don't clearly understand words and I must guess at what people are saying. Sometimes, I must focus on what is being said and use all my mental energy engaged in a conversation so I can hear what people are saying, especially if there is a lot of background noise.

This was not one of those times. The only background noise was the shuffling about of different people making final preparations for the concert. Our group was small, so there wasn't much conversational noise. There was no reason for me to misunderstand when our tour guide said, "You can all have a turn sitting at Elton John's piano."

This was the moment I was never so happy to be debt-free. This concert was the fifth I had attended since becoming debt-free, but it was the most epic adventure—traveling to New York City and attending a concert on New Year's Eve. Money no longer stood in between me and pursuing my dream.

For the past twenty-two years, my dream had been to meet Elton John in person. And now, I'd get to sit at his piano. That's the closest I have come to achieving my goal.

As I processed the guide's directions, I noticed that no one had moved to start the photo session. It was as if an invisible fence wrapped around the piano and no one wanted to go first and open the invisible gate that would give everyone else in our group permission to follow. The tour guide said something to the effect of, "Someone has to go first, and you better hurry or else we won't have time to get this done." Someone stepped forward we all followed in line.

As my turn neared, I couldn't believe what was happening. Careful to not touch the piano, I slid sideways onto the bench and just looked—his piano keys, his microphone, the set list taped to just above the left side of the keys—it was all there, right in front of me. I had given the tour guide my phone and turned to pose for the camera. Tommy was taking pictures, too, so I turned to look at him as well.

Thinking back on this moment, I'm reminded of the quote that goes something like this: "Money doesn't buy happiness, but it can buy experiences, and experiences make you happy!"

At that moment, sitting at Elton's piano, I had to take a few minutes and let the moment sink in. This was happening! I was debt-free and sitting at Elton John's piano. Was sitting at Elton John's piano my biggest dream? No, but it was one step closer—the closest I have gotten—and I wasn't going to pass up the opportunity.

The tour continued toward Jon Mahon's percussion kit, down the side stage stairs, and to a little workshop area set up for guitar guy. We were introduced to several guitars, one of them the *Mandolisa*. It's a beautiful mandolin with a hand-painted scene depicting the New York City skyline and a caricature. Guitar guy explained his job—to care for, repair, and prep every guitar (I forget how many there were)—but each one had its own velvet-lined slot in a huge travel box that closes like a clamshell. He took a few more out to show us and explained the details. They are so beautiful on stage, but even more exquisite up close. We were each given a token guitar pick during this part of the tour, as well as the opportunity to take photos of the guitars. Again, not allowed to touch!

After the on-stage part of the tour, we were taken behind the stage and down a long hallway to the green room. The hallway was lined with travel boxes used to transport the equipment. Some of the boxes had stenciled names on them; some did not. There are so many, and they are huge. No wonder it takes so many tractor trailers to transport everything.

Once in the green room, we were instructed to stay there, enjoy the food and drink provided, and just hang out. I wanted to wander around backstage, but I also knew that there are security guards everywhere, and I wanted *more* not to be escorted out of the building than I wanted to wander around, so I stay put. We mixed and mingled with the other people in the room, and I met a couple named Randy and Nancy who have been to twenty-nine concerts. This concert was number thirty for them. I also met the editor of *EltonJohn.com*, although I didn't know who he was until he introduced himself. I didn't recognize his face, but I certainly recognized his name. He was wearing a pin with the logo for the *Two Low for Zero* album and I commented on it. He was impressed I knew what it meant.

At one point, I heard some commotion in the hallway, so I went over to the doorway and peeked out. I noticed that some of the other folks from the tour had ended up in the hallway and were talking to Davey Johnstone. I thought since they were in the hallway, I should go out there too, and that is where I met Davey and had my photo taken with him. It was awesome. He was so down-to-earth and humble, and took the time to autograph the sheet I had brought just for the occasion. What I remember most is saying to him is, "It's such an honor to meet you."

His reply was simple and humble: "Oh? I'm just a guitar player, blessed to be able to do what I do."

I was reminded of the conversation with guitar guy from earlier. First, Davey Johnstone was not just any guitar player. He is one of the original members of the Elton John band and has been playing with Elton for many, many years. He is Davey Johnstone! But, he doesn't see himself that way. To him, he is a guitar player, doing what he loves to do: play guitar. And, wow, does he ever love to play that guitar. It's so evident watching him play during a concert. I'm sure it's just a bonus that he gets to share the stage with Elton John. I'm sure that, to Davey, Elton is just a piano player.

After meeting Davey, we also had the opportunity to meet

the other members of the band. Eventually, we were all kindly instructed to go back in the green room and one by one, Jon, Kim, Nigel, and Matt came in to hang out with all of us.

So, yes, there we were in the green room hanging out with other fans, the editor of *EltonJohn.com*, and the members of the band. Just hanging out and chatting like regular people. Like it was an ordinary evening cocktail party. It was surreal, but cool at the same time. Every member of the band took the time to visit with each one of us, give autographs, and pose for pictures. They were genuinely humbled to learn most of us traveled from great distances to be there. They were just as excited to see us there as we were to see them.

About fifteen minutes before the concert began, we left the green room to go to our seats. A band called Bright Lights, Bright Lights opened the show, which is a rarity for Elton. I heard their last two songs and wasn't impressed. I wasn't there to see them; I was there to see Elton. Honestly, I was annoyed there was an opening act, but I appreciate that Elton gave some young musical artists a chance to open for him. That is something that so rarely happens; in my concert experience it's only happened twice, once with 2Cellos and once with Bright Lights, Bright Lights.

Around 9:00 p.m., the opening act finished their set. A flurry of activity on the stage meant their musical equipment was loaded off, and my excitement grew as the real concert was about to begin.

The concert began like any other, with the familiar notes of the introduction to *Funeral for a Friend.* The crowd energy was amazing; I could feel the excitement from all around the venue. Elton John walked out in the brightest, fire engine-red suit I have ever seen and kicked off the show. He played what I now consider a normal set list—the hits and a few new songs— until just before midnight. A few seconds before midnight, Elton began to count down, "Three, two, one! Happy New Year!"

The crowd erupted in celebration; red and white balloons dropped from the ceiling and ticker-tape confetti flew everywhere. After a few minutes of celebration, Elton asked from the microphone, "Where's my family?" and proceeded to tell the crowd that James and Haley got engaged. He asked them to join him on stage and introduced them to the crowd. What a great moment to be there and witness that.

Elton returned to the piano and began to sing "Don't Let the Sun Go Down on Me;" what a song to just stop and reflect on what just happened. I was at the Barclay Center in Brooklyn, New York, and I had just celebrated the New Year with nineteen thousand Elton John fans.

The lyrics of the song caused me to stop and reflect in the midst of the concert chaos. Taking the chance on getting better with money led me to a debt-free life. Taking the chance to pursue my dream when it didn't seem possible led me to opportunities I would never have imagined. Taking the chance on asking a group of women for advice on a shirt, and then taking the additional chance of purchasing the recommended shirt even though it was totally outside my comfort zone led to another amazing experience.

After singing "Don't Let the Sun Go Down on Me," Elton explained to the audience that there would be a live cut-in from *Dick Clark's Rocking New Year's Eve* hosted by Ryan Seacrest. The next few minutes of the concert would be broadcast on national TV. The set list continued with rousing renditions of "I'm Still Standing," "Your Sister Can't Twist," and "Saturday Night's Alright for Fighting."

During these songs, Davey Johnstone played a few guitar solos and walked right up to the edge of the stage and placed guitar picks right into the hands of some lucky fans. I know this because not only have I witnessed it, but I have been that lucky recipient on more than one occasion. I know the routine: get as close to the stage as possible, stick my hand as far up in the air as I can get it toward the stage, and make eye contact. So, that's exactly what I did.

What I didn't know was that because of the live remote, there were static cameras placed throughout the venue. These cameras were on long poles and controlled through a remote operator. One of these was placed near the far end of the stage and panned the audience during one of Davey's walks to the edge of the stage. Although I didn't receive a guitar pick at this concert, I did have a unique, memorable experience—my arm was on national TV!

Yes, that long-sleeve, sparkly, sequined shirt stood out on national TV when the camera zoomed in on Davey. I had no idea what was happening at the time, or else I would have turned towards the camera and waved.

I didn't know about my famous arm until after the concert when I checked my phone. It had blown up with messages from friends who'd seen it on TV. I can't believe I had no idea what was happening. Fortunately for me, several friends had this recording on their DVR and could capture screen shots and send them to me.

This show is on my top ten list of all-time favorite concert experiences. Never could I have imagined that I would have worn a silver, sparkly, sequined shirt; had the opportunity to sit at Elton's piano; meet every member of the band; and have a second-row seat to a New Year's Eve celebration in the midst of nineteen thousand people. In addition, I met Nancy and Randy, who would later join me in other concert adventures.

Life Lesson:
Go big or stay home. This was such a special occasion it required I go all out for this one, including stepping way outside of my comfort zone in many ways.

30
That's Not Good Enough

September 2016
Savannah, GA

My trip to Savannah to see Elton John at the Savannah Civic Center was perhaps the easiest of the four trips in September to plan. I would make the five-hour drive from home, leave the day before the concert, and drive home the following day.

I bought a ninth-row ticket the day the tickets went on sale through Ticketmaster. I then bought a fourth-row ticket about a month before the concert and sold the ninth-row ticket. Everything just came together logistically for this concert. It was almost too easy.

The only problem was that I was in the fourth row. Now, before you get irritated with me because I am a seat snob, keep in mind that I am attending concerts because I am pursuing the dream of meeting Elton John in person. Yes, of course I love attending the concerts, but if I don't sit close, he won't know I'm there. Also, many venues only let the first three rows go up to the stage when Elton gives out autographs, so again, it's important that I am up close.

This was also the first of four concerts I was attending, so I had to be careful about the budget. At this point in my life, I was debt-free and cash-flowing my trips. I only had the amount of money in my budget that I had saved up until leaving for the concert, so I had to manage how much money I spent to sit up close. I decided that fourth row for Savannah would be okay because I wanted to save money for the concert in Allentown,

Pennsylvania, which would be on my birthday.

Usually when I arrive at the venue and find my seat, I seek out the people I have come to know who work for Elton John. They may or may not always remember my name, but they recognize me. I don't take up much of their time because they are working, but I wave and maybe have a quick bit of small talk with them. If I'm lucky, there may be a member of the band hanging around on the side of the stage and I can give him a quick wave as well. After all, they are just as important to the concert as the man himself. I always enjoy meeting the truck drivers, the van drivers, the techs, and anyone else involved in making the show happen.

On this particular night, one of these people was interacting with the fans right before and during the concert. I saw him walking around the front part of the stage and, because I was standing near the front row chatting with friends, I got his attention. When he acknowledged me, I said hello and then, very sarcastically, "Oh, I'm sitting *all the way* back there, in the fourth row."

He laughed along with my sarcasm; he understands that a real, true fan doesn't want to sit all the way back in the fourth row.

While I'm not exactly sure what he does, I knew he had a million things to do before the concert began, so I didn't keep him long. He walked off to the other area near the stage and, at about the same time, I received a message from a friend of mine who was sitting in the tiered section of the venue. I decided to walk up there to say hello.

I wasn't gone very long because it was almost show time, and I knew I needed to be in my seat at least five minutes before 8:00 because that's when the entire venue goes black. As I made my way back to my seat, I stopped once again to visit with my friends in the front row. As I stood there, I saw someone walking toward me out of the corner of my eye. But before I could turn around I heard, "This is extra! You are now in the second row!" and simultaneously felt a paper ticket being placed in my hand. It was all so sudden that it took me longer to process what had happened than it did for me to formulate a very grateful thank you, and then he was gone.

Regardless, at that moment, I became a second-row seat fan. I now had two tickets. With very little time left, I walked to the tier of people above the floor, found someone sitting by herself, and gave her my fourth-row ticket. She was happy; I was happy; it was a win-win!

I returned to my new seat and, once again, anxiously waited for the house lights to go off and watch Elton John ascend to the stage. He waved to the crowd and sat just seconds before joining in with the band on the opening song.

From my seat, I could see from his chin to the top of his head just over the top of that true concert grand piano—no electronic instrument for Elton! I could watch him play from the large projector screens overhead, although I can't look at those too long because of the way they are angled; they are not meant for people in the first few rows to look at. I do it anyway because I love to just watch him play, especially during the mini piano solos before and in the middle of songs. That's something you just don't get from buying and album or CD.

Throughout the concert, I sang and danced as best as I could in the second row. There's not much room in between the rows, but if I'm lucky, the seat flips up. I stand almost the entire concert, except during slow songs like "Daniel." That's when I give myself a little break and sit down for a while. I listen to the crowd sing along; I watch the band; I take in everything happening around me. I love every single part of the entire concert experience.

Elton played for almost two and a half hours. The crowd was energetic, but not the most energetic I've ever seen. Many people sat for the entire show. When it was time, I made my way to my spot at the end of the stage. Elton began playing the encore and Jon Mahon, the percussionist, walked right over to our area. He clapped and played the tambourine and got the crowd involved in the song. I had put my poster, the one I made that read "My 33rd Concert," on the edge of the stage. Jon walked over to it, read it and, picked it up to show to the crowd. I was so excited I couldn't get a picture right away; it was as if I totally forgot how to take a picture with my iPhone. Just as he was going to put the poster back on the stage I yelled out, "Wait! One more try!" and he so graciously paused and posed with my poster to be sure I got a good picture.

Just before the encore, Elton John walked from one end of the stage to the other to acknowledge the crowd. On his way back to the piano, he gave out autographs. This part of the concert has become routine for me, but it's still nerve-wracking and exciting. It's a gamble whether he chooses to sign something or not, regardless of what anyone brings to get signed. This time, I chose to bring my 40th Anniversary Collector's Edition of *Goodbye Yellow Brick Road*. It was the first album (in the form of the cassette tape) that I ever listened to. There were so many people clambering to get his autograph and holding up all types of things to get signed. I stood there, holding the set high above my head, stretching my arm toward the stage and, for good measure, rose on my tippy toes and joined in the chant to get his attention:

"Elton! Elton!" I yelled.

His assistant/security guard scanned the crowd, looking for items.

He saw what I held up in my hands, we made eye contact for

a brief moment, and he leaned over and grabbed it, handed it to Elton and I received another autograph!

"Thank you!" I yelled. I wasn't sure if he could hear me, but just in case he did, I wanted him to know how appreciative I was that he chose my item to sign.

As Elton moved across the stage, I decided to move, too. I wanted to be on the outside fringe of the crowd in front of the piano so I could see the back of his jacket and maybe, just maybe, get an extra nod or a wave as he exited the stage after the last song.

Everything, at this point, was about the strategy to get his attention. It wasn't enough that I just got his autograph, and obviously, he saw me standing there at the edge of the stage. I needed to be sure he knew I was there, that I didn't just get lost in the sea of people. It was a little bit of a pre-thought process, but mostly I was thinking on my feet and taking advantage of any opportunity that came along.

The set list on this particular night included *Candle in the Wind* after the autograph session. I realized how amazing it was to stand there and not only watch Elton sing and play, but to look out at the crowd as one by one, and then group by group, the fans turned on the flashlight app on their phones and held them up. Some people waved the light from side to side; some just held it up. Soon, almost every fan in the sold-out arena had a light shining and it was a beautiful sight to watch come to life.

Elton stood up to acknowledge the crowd one last time before hitting the first few notes of "Crocodile Rock," a song everyone knew, and the crowd cheered along. One of my favorite parts of this song live in concert is the crowd sing-a-long during the "la, la la la la la" part. Elton comes out from behind the piano and "conducts" the crowd. Almost everyone joins in; how could they not? Hearing eleven thousand people join in on a sing-a-long is quite loud, but Elton loves it. On this night, the more the crowd participated, the more he interacted and fed off the energy.

With one final note and one final slam of the piano key cover against the piano, the concert ended in dramatic fashion. Elton walked off the stage to the thunderous applause of the energized crowd. He descended the steps to the floor and proceeded to the side entrance. The house lights came on, the stage hands appeared to start disassembling the instruments, and the ushers began asking as to leave the arena.

We lingered as long as we could, not wanting the entire experience to be over, but not wanting to be escorted out of the building. After all, the instruments and the set needed to be on the next stop and the ushers were ready to go home.

Life Lesson:
Be content with what you have, but let people know what you want.

31
My Not-So-Ordinary Life

Present Day 2017

My life seems so ordinary at this point. I've been married for over fifteen years; we have two boys and four dogs. We own a home and we each have our own vehicle (with no payments). My husband works for a major corporation and I own my own business. My husband is a salaried employee and I, well, I'm an entrepreneur. There is no such thing as a regular paycheck with predictable, steady profit four years into my business venture. Much of the profit I earn gets invested back into growing the business. That's okay, though, because we have created a financial life to support this method. We are debt-free except for the mortgage. This is the life we have created and this is our normal.

Do you read any of that and think to yourself, "Wow! That's extraordinary!"

In so many ways, we are the typical American family, and in many ways, we are not. Many times, I forget the lesson I learned from guitar guy, because things that are extraordinary to you are such a normal part of my day-to-day life. I'll admit this chapter of the book is hard for me to share because I feel like I'm bragging or tooting my own horn, and it's hard for me to do that. But I think it's important to share because we do need to remember this lesson about living our own extraordinary lives and understanding that what is ordinary to us is extraordinary to others. Our ordinary lives can be such an inspiration to others.

"We've been married for sixteen years," I say.

"Wow! Congratulations; that's awesome!" someone will respond.

Really? Well, yes, it is awesome. I have been married to the *same person* for sixteen years. Today, that's quite an accomplishment. I don't think it's an extraordinary event. I went into this relationship knowing I was going to marry my husband and knowing that it would, indeed, be until death do us part. I know many people whose marriages do not make it to sixteen years, and I know many people who have been married longer.

What's so extraordinary about a sixteen-year marriage? There are many times that we haven't liked each other very much, but our marriage is built on a foundation of love. It's okay that we don't like each other from time to time. People change. My husband is not the same person I married fifteen years ago, and I'm not the same person he married. I like to think we have changed for the better, and I know he would agree. Change is hard, and since we individually grow through change, then our marriage must grow through that change. We do that by choosing each day to be together, to be married, and work through the good and the bad. Neither one of us is perfect, but we are perfect for each other.

There are so many things I say now that just roll off my tongue like any other person would say "peanut butter sandwich." These things are so ordinary to me, but because I forget they are extraordinary to other people, I say them like it's no big deal.

"We paid off over $43,000 of debt in less than four years."

"Our boys are thirteen months apart."

"I've seen Elton John thirty-six times in concert."

"I got Elton John's autograph!"

"I am an entrepreneur."

"We have four dogs."

Each of these things by themselves are extraordinary statements. Not everyone can say those things and have them be true. I can. These things, by themselves, have inspired other people to do the same or similar. These statements have given people hope and courage and yes, put ideas into their heads. I recognize that I live an extraordinary life. But, it's only because I chose to do that.

Life Lesson:
Your normal is someone else's goal; help them get there.

Epilogue

March 2017

It's been a long time since that first concert in 1992. In many ways, I've done more in the last twenty-four years than most people do in an entire lifetime. While I'm in the process of living day-to-day-life, I forget all that I have accomplished. Writing this book has helped me remember that.

For years, I would share my stories of these epic Elton John concert adventures and people would always tell me, "You should write a book!" It took me a long time to listen.

Who was I to write a book? I'm not an author. I'm not a writer. Maybe I'll just jot down some notes to tell later when the time comes to share stories. That's all well and good, except that there will come a time when I am no longer around to tell the stories. That is the driving force behind this book. I wanted to have all the stories in one place. I started writing in 2014 and called this document *DreamBook2014*. This is the story of how my dream came to be and what I have done to pursue it. Not every decision was the right decision to get me closer to my dream, but I've learned that I've made more right decisions than wrong ones. The more I pursued my dream, the more I wanted to pursue it. I am driven by all the people who doubted, who called my dream crazy, and yes, who questioned my sanity in pursuing it.

It takes some sort of crazy to pursue a dream. That is a lesson in itself. Not everyone can do it. Most people have dreams, but not everyone pursues them. I didn't want to be one of *those* people. My entire life is a dichotomy of opposites; I might as well embrace it.

Most importantly, I want this to be a story for my boys. Some days, I'm just trying to keep them alive and not permanently grounded (their consequence for poor behavior). Other days, I'm talking to them about their goals and dreams and encouraging them to pursue those. They are only eleven and ten, but all they have ever known is that, "Mommy goes to see Elton John." Do they know why? They do, but I'm not sure they fully understand.

This book started out as a book of stories, written as I remembered them when I sat down to write. Initially, it was stories from each concert I attended. Then, I applied to speak at a conference and was accepted. My speech was titled, "Life Lessons from Pursuing a Dream," and I told the story of how I met Valerie at that concert in Roanoke, Virginia, in 1999. With that speech, I wanted to do more than share a story. I wanted to leave the audience with some actionable steps they could immediate apply in their own lives. Those actionable steps are identified in this book as *life lessons*. The speech was so well received that it changed the way this book was written. It's *not* just a book of concert stories. In the words of Elton, "Each day I learn just a little bit more; I don't know why but I do know what for…"

I know the life lessons I have learned.

I know they were meant to be implemented and shared.

The one question everyone asks, "Have you met Elton yet?"

No, not yet. The closest I have gotten was a handshake from the stage at the concert in Wilkes-Barre, Pennsylvania, on September 24, 2016. I was right up against the stage in front of the piano, and when Elton came to the side of the stage, he shook my hand, as well as all the others that were raised high above our heads for that purpose.

Although I haven't met him yet, I know one day I will. So far, I've gotten that handshake, sat at his piano, and met every member of his band. I know Elton recognizes me and my RKTMNFAN license plate. I can see it in his face when he looks out into the crowd and sees me standing there with the picture of my license plate and recently, my bright green neon poster.

On September 27, 2016, I attended my thirty-sixth Elton John concert. It was also our third-year anniversary of being debt-free and my forty-third birthday. This book ends with that epic concert run in late September 2016—Savannah, Hershey, Wilkes-Barre, and Allentown. Four concerts in eight days. I was in the first three rows for each, the last being my birthday. I celebrated that day in the *front row* thanks to a little help from a friend. And yes, I cash flowed the entire trip.

For now, I don't have any concert trips planned. My bucket list includes a trip to Vegas for the Million Dollar Piano show, and I'm sure that will be just an epic of an adventure as all the other concerts. Who knows, maybe I'll land someplace super fun for my fortieth concert, which will be significant because I was debt-free on my fortieth birthday.

Until then, I just keep learning life lessons with each concert I attend. I keep meeting new people and having new, epic adventures. I've been told I inspire people, too, in the pursuit of their dreams. I hadn't intended for that to happen, but I'm glad it did. I hope you will make a list of your dreams too, and start making plans toward achieving them. Even if you don't achieve them, you'll have some great stories to tell. Who knows, you may even learn some of your own life lessons along the way.

My Elton John Concert List

1. August 1992 Raleigh, NC

2. May 1993 Chapel Hill, NC

3. April 1995 Columbia, SC

4. August 1995 Raleigh, NC

5. September 1995 Charlotte, NC

6. October 1998 Chapel Hill, NC

7. October 1998 Charlotte, NC

8. September 1998 Bristow, VA

9. February 1999 Roanoke, VA

10. April 2001 Charlotte, NC

11. November 2003 Norfolk, VA

12. July 2004 Radio City Music Hall, New York, NY

13. November 2005 Winston-Salem, NC

14. November 2007 Charleston, SC

15. May 2007 Greenville, SC

16. April 2008 Radio City Music Hall, New York, NY

17. March 2009 Charlotte, NC

The following took place during our debt-free journey:

18. November 2010 Asheville, NC

19. March 15, 2012 Roanoke, VA

20. March 16, 2012 Raleigh, NC

21. March 17, 2012 Richmond, VA

22. April 2013 Winston-Salem, NC

The following took place after becoming debt-free:

23. November 2013 Washington, DC

24. November 2013 Atlanta, GA

25. June 2014 Charleston, WV

26. June 2014 Charlotte, NC

27. December 31, 2014 Brooklyn, NY

28. March 11, 2015 Fayetteville, NC

29. March 13, 2015 Greenville, SC

30. March 2016 Roanoke, VA

31. March 2016 Charlottesville, VA

32. March 2016 Youngstown, OH

33. September 2016 Savannah, GA

34. September 2016 Hershey, PA

35. September 2016 Wilkes-Barre, PA

36. September 2016 Allentown, PA

Acknowledgements

This is the hardest page to write because I hope and pray I leave no one out.

Above all else, I thank God for giving me this dream to pursue. It hasn't always been easy, but it has been worth it. Thank you, God, for putting the right people in the right place at the right time and giving me the tools I need to pursue this dream. Thank you for being patient with me as You show me your path for me. Thank you for your grace, your protection and choosing this life for me.

To my husband, Jack, who didn't run away when I told him one of my goals in life was to meet Elton John. Thank you for loving me anyway and always supporting this endeavor by saying, "Yes, dear," anytime I hand you a slip of paper for the dates you need to put in for vacation from work. Thank you for using your vacation days to allow me to pursue my dream.

Thank you for supporting my crazy ideas even if, at first, you may not always agree or be on board. I love you most for your patience in living with a wife who has big dreams, and always being supportive. Thank you for always allowing me to be me and for us to be us.

To my parents, who instilled a love of music at an early age. Especially to my dad, who bought that *Goodbye Yellow Brick Road* cassette and allowed me the opportunity to peruse through it that fateful day. What a journey that one cassette tape started!

To all my family members and friends who have attended Elton John concerts with me and those who have graciously listened to my stories. I am so grateful to have shared my love of the concert with you and to have you join me in that experience.

To Valerie, thank you for taking the time that day in Roanoke to meet me and change the course of this journey. Many of these epic adventures would never have happened if I hadn't met you. Thank you for helping me with my memory as I wrote this book, and for saving my emails. I hope we enjoy many more concert adventures together!

To all my Elton concert friends, thank you for being fans and being my friends. You are the reason I know this isn't some crazy dream. Thank you for being "my people" and making every concert experience we have had together that much more memorable and enjoyable!

To Katrina, thank you for introducing me to Financial Peace University and changing our lives forever.

To Holly, thank you for being the second of three nudges I needed to start my business. Thank you for always supporting and encouraging me along the way.

To Daniel "Rudy" Reuttiger, thank you for writing your autobiography and, ultimately, being the final inspiration I needed to start my business.

To the Dreamers and Builders Community (including subgroups), you all are the best supporters I know. Thank you for pursuing your dreams and giving me the courage to pursue mine. Many of you have gone out of your way to help me in various aspects of my journey. I will be forever grateful for your kindness and support.

Thank you to the Elton John band (including 2Cellos, Tata Vega, Rose Stone, Lisa Stone and Jean Witherspoon), who always take the time out to meet fans, whether it's backstage, in a hotel lobby, or the backstage parking lot before the concert. You are the kindest, most gracious and humble people I have ever met. Thank you for always putting on a great experience every time you take the concert stage. It is my honor to have met you and to watch you work together.

To my Book Team:

Anna Floit, my editor — you believed in my story from the beginning. You helped take words and sentences on paper and turn them into a cohesive story with proper sentence structure, grammar, etc. I am so grateful for your friendship and expertise! *www.annafloit.com*

Haley Walden, my proofreader — you were the extra set of eyes to make sure everything was just right. *www.haleywalden.com*

Lindsey Hartz, my marketing consultant — your expertise helped me learn how to share my story with my circle of influence. Your encouragement and accountability throughout the process are so greatly appreciated. *www.lindseyhartz.com*

Scott Cuzzo — my graphic design guru. Thank you for helping develop my vision for the cover into a beautiful work of art. Your expertise in all things involving Createspace was so valuable to me through this process. *www.scottcuzzo.com*

To everyone on the book launch team and those of you who shared my story, purchased a book and told your friends to buy one too! Your support is so greatly appreciated and I thank you!

Finally, thank you to Sir Elton John, for showing us all what a life headed in the right direction can look like. Thank you for not quitting on yourself or your career in the early days. Thank you for maintaining your songwriting relationship with Bernie Taupin and creating more albums. For taking on new projects like Broadway and the movies. Thank you for always putting on the best show when you are sitting behind that concert grand piano. Thank you for indulging this fan in countless autographs and acknowledgements from the stage. And I'll take the time here to thank you in advance for taking the time to meet me and make this dream I've had since 1992 come true. You are truly a legend and an inspiration.

Made in the USA
Columbia, SC
06 September 2017